Collyer

Square Measure at a Glance

Collyer

Square Measure at a Glance

ISBN/EAN: 9783337713492

Printed in Europe, USA, Canada, Australia, Japan

Cover: Foto ©ninafisch / pixelio.de

More available books at **www.hansebooks.com**

QUARE MEASURE AT A GLANCE.

LYER'S TABLES FOR CALCULATING SUPERFICIAL AREAS.

PREFACE.

WE have for many years used the following Calculating Tables, in a manuscript form, in our own business, for ascertaining the superficial area of blinds with rapidity and ease, and finding that no similar work has hitherto been published or is obtainable, we feel sure that this work will be of great use to all connected with the Building Trade, and who require to calculate the areas of large numbers of windows or other superficial measurement.

These Tables being from 1-ft. 6-in. × 13-ft. 0-in., rising every inch to 5-ft. 11-in. × 13-ft. 0-in., include all the usual widths and heights of windows, and we have endeavoured by carefully checking the calculations to ensure the utmost correctness.

'C. COLLYER & SON.

January, 1879.

1-ft. 6-in.

1-ft. 6-in. by			1-ft. 6-in. by			1-ft. 6-in. by		
ft. in.	ft. in.	pts.	ft. in.	ft. in.	pts.	ft. in.	ft. in.	pts.
1 6 =	2 3	0	5 5 =	8 1	6	9 4 =	14 0	0
1 7	2 4	6	5 6	8 3	0	9 5	14 1	6
1 8	2 6	0	5 7	8 4	6	9 6	14 3	0
1 9	2 7	6	5 8	8 6	0	9 7	14 4	6
1 10	2 9	0	5 9	8 7	6	9 8	14 6	0
1 11	2 10	6	5 10	8 9	0	9 9	14 7	6
2 0	3 0	0	5 11	8 10	6	9 10	14 9	0
2 1	3 1	6	6 0	9 0	0	9 11	14 10	6
2 2	3 3	0	6 1	9 1	6	10 0	15 0	0
2 3	3 4	6	6 2	9 3	0	10 1	15 1	6
2 4	3 6	0	6 3	9 4	6	10 2	15 3	0
2 5	3 7	6	6 4	9 6	0	10 3	15 4	6
2 6	3 9	0	6 5	9 7	6	10 4	15 6	0
2 7	3 10	6	6 6	9 9	0	10 5	15 7	6
2 8	4 0	0	6 7	9 10	6	10 6	15 9	0
2 9	4 1	6	6 8	10 0	0	10 7	15 10	6
2 10	4 3	0	6 9	10 1	6	10 8	16 0	0
2 11	4 4	6	6 10	10 3	0	10 9	16 1	6
3 0	4 6	0	6 11	10 4	6	10 10	16 3	0
3 1	4 7	6	7 0	10 6	0	10 11	16 4	6
3 2	4 9	0	7 1	10 7	6	11 0	16 6	0
3 3	4 10	6	7 2	10 9	0	11 1	16 7	6
3 4	5 0	0	7 3	10 10	6	11 2	16 9	0
3 5	5 1	6	7 4	11 0	0	11 3	16 10	6
3 6	5 3	0	7 5	11 1	6	11 4	17 0	0
3 7	5 4	6	7 6	11 3	0	11 5	17 1	6
3 8	5 6	0	7 7	11 4	6	11 6	17 3	0
3 9	5 7	6	7 8	11 6	0	11 7	17 4	6
3 10	5 9	0	7 9	11 7	6	11 8	17 6	0
3 11	5 10	6	7 10	11 9	0	11 9	17 7	6
4 0	6 0	0	7 11	11 10	6	11 10	17 9	0
4 1	6 1	6	8 0	12 0	0	11 11	17 10	6
4 2	6 3	0	8 1	12 1	6	12 0	18 0	0
4 3	6 4	6	8 2	12 3	0	12 1	18 1	6
4 4	6 6	0	8 3	12 4	6	12 2	18 3	0
4 5	6 7	6	8 4	12 6	0	12 3	18 4	6
4 6	6 9	0	8 5	12 7	6	12 4	18 6	0
4 7	6 10	6	8 6	12 9	0	12 5	18 7	6
4 8	7 0	0	8 7	12 10	6	12 6	18 9	0
4 9	7 1	6	8 8	13 0	0	12 7	18 10	6
4 10	7 3	0	8 9	13 1	6	12 8	19 0	0
4 11	7 4	6	8 10	13 3	0	12 9	19 1	6
5 0	7 6	0	8 11	13 4	6	12 10	19 3	0
5 1	7 7	6	9 0	13 6	0	12 11	19 4	6
5 2	7 9	0	9 1	13 7	6	13 0	19 6	0
5 3	7 10	6	9 2	13 9	0			
5 4	8 0	0	9 3	13 10	6			

1-ft. 7-in.

ft. in.	ft. in. pts.	ft. in.	ft. in. pts.	ft. in.	ft. in. pts.
1-ft. 7-in. by		1-ft. 7-in. by		1-ft. 7-in. by	
1 6	= 2 4 6	5 5	= 8 6 11	9 4	14 9 4
1 7	2 6 1	5 6	8 8 6	9 5	14 10 11
1 8	2 7 8	5 7	8 10 1	9 6	15 0 6
1 9	2 9 3	5 8	8 11 8	9 7	15 2 1
1 10	2 10 10	5 9	9 1 3	9 8	15 3 8
1 11	3 0 5	5 10	9 2 10	9 9	15 5 3
2 0	3 2 0	5 11	9 4 5	9 10	15 6 10
2 1	3 3 7	6 0	9 6 0	9 11	15 8 5
2 2	3 5 2	6 1	9 7 7	10 0	15 10 0
2 3	3 6 9	6 2	9 9 2	10 1	15 11 7
2 4	3 8 4	6 3	9 10 9	10 2	16 1 2
2 5	3 9 11	6 4	10 0 4	10 3	16 2 9
2 6	3 11 6	6 5	10 1 11	10 4	16 4 4
2 7	4 1 1	6 6	10 3 6	10 5	16 5 11
2 8	4 2 8	6 7	10 5 1	10 6	16 7 6
2 9	4 4 3	6 8	10 6 8	10 7	16 9 1
2 10	4 5 10	6 9	10 8 3	10 8	16 10 8
2 11	4 7 5	6 10	10 9 10	10 9	17 0 3
3 0	4 9 0	6 11	10 11 5	10 10	17 1 10
3 1	4 10 7	7 0	11 1 0	10 11	17 3 5
3 2	5 0 2	7 1	11 2 7	11 0	17 5 0
3 3	5 1 9	7 2	11 4 2	11 1	17 6 7
3 4	5 3 4	7 3	11 5 9	11 2	17 8 2
3 5	5 4 11	7 4	11 7 4	11 3	17 9 9
3 6	5 6 6	7 5	11 8 11	11 4	17 11 4
3 7	5 8 1	7 6	11 10 6	11 5	18 0 11
3 8	5 9 8	7 7	12 0 1	11 6	18 2 6
3 9	5 11 3	7 8	12 1 8	11 7	18 4 1
3 10	6 0 10	7 9	12 3 3	11 8	18 5 8
3 11	6 2 5	7 10	12 4 10	11 9	18 7 3
4 0	6 4 0	7 11	12 6 5	11 10	18 8 10
4 1	6 5 7	8 0	12 8 0	11 11	18 10 5
4 2	6 7 2	8 1	12 9 7	12 0	19 0 0
4 3	6 8 9	8 2	12 11 2	12 1	19 1 7
4 4	6 10 4	8 3	13 0 9	12 2	19 3 2
4 5	6 11 11	8 4	13 2 4	12 3	19 4 9
4 6	7 1 6	8 5	13 3 11	12 4	19 6 4
4 7	7 3 1	8 6	13 5 6	12 5	19 7 11
4 8	7 4 8	8 7	13 7 1	12 6	19 9 6
4 9	7 6 3	8 8	13 8 8	12 7	19 11 1
4 10	7 7 10	8 9	13 10 3	12 8	20 0 8
4 11	7 9 5	8 10	13 11 10	12 9	20 2 3
5 0	7 11 0	8 11	14 1 5	12 10	20 3 10
5 1	8 0 7	9 0	14 3 0	12 11	20 5 5
5 2	8 2 2	9 1	14 4 7	13 0	20 7 0
5 3	8 3 9	9 2	14 6 2		
5 4	8 5 4	9 3	14 7 9		

1-ft. 8-in.

1-ft. 8-in. by				1-ft. 8-in. by				1-ft. 8-in. by			
ft.	in.	ft.	in. pts.	ft.	in.	ft.	in. pts.	ft.	in.	ft.	in. pts.
1	6	= 2	6 0	5	5	= 9	0 4	9	4	=15	6 8
1	7	2	7 8	5	6	9	2 0	9	5	15	8 4
1	8	2	9 4	5	7	9	3 8	9	6	15	10 0
1	9	2	11 0	5	8	9	5 4	9	7	15	11 8
1	10	3	0 8	5	9	9	7 0	9	8	16	1 4
1	11	3	2 4	5	10	9	8 8	9	9	16	3 0
2	0	3	4 0	5	11	9	10 4	9	10	16	4 8
2	1	3	5 8	6	0	10	0 0	9	11	16	6 4
2	2	3	7 4	6	1	10	1 8	10	0	16	8 0
2	3	3	9 0	6	2	10	3 4	10	1	16	9 8
2	4	3	10 8	6	3	10	5 0	10	2	16	11 4
2	5	4	0 4	6	4	10	6 8	10	3	17	1 0
2	6	4	2 0	6	5	10	8 4	10	4	17	2 8
2	7	4	3 8	6	6	10	10 0	10	5	17	4 4
2	8	4	5 4	6	7	10	11 8	10	6	17	6 0
2	9	4	7 0	6	8	11	1 4	10	7	17	7 8
2	10	4	8 8	6	9	11	3 0	10	8	17	9 4
2	11	4	10 4	6	10	11	4 8	10	9	17	11 0
3	0	5	0 0	6	11	11	6 4	10	10	18	0 8
3	1	5	1 8	7	0	11	8 0	10	11	18	2 4
3	2	5	3 4	7	1	11	9 8	11	0	18	4 0
3	3	5	5 0	7	2	11	11 4	11	1	18	5 8
3	4	5	6 8	7	3	12	1 0	11	2	18	7 4
3	5	5	8 4	7	4	12	2 8	11	3	18	9 0
3	6	5	10 0	7	5	12	4 4	11	4	18	10 8
3	7	5	11 8	7	6	12	6 0	11	5	19	0 4
3	8	6	1 4	7	7	12	7 8	11	6	19	2 0
3	9	6	3 0	7	8	12	9 4	11	7	19	3 8
3	10	6	4 8	7	9	12	11 0	11	8	19	5 4
3	11	6	6 4	7	10	13	0 8	11	9	19	7 0
4	0	6	8 0	7	11	13	2 4	11	10	19	8 8
4	1	6	9 8	8	0	13	4 0	11	11	19	10 4
4	2	6	11 4	8	1	13	5 8	12	0	20	0 0
4	3	7	1 0	8	2	13	7 4	12	1	20	1 8
4	4	7	2 8	8	3	13	9 0	12	2	20	3 4
4	5	7	4 4	8	4	13	10 8	12	3	20	5 0
4	6	7	6 0	8	5	14	0 4	12	4	20	6 8
4	7	7	7 8	8	6	14	2 0	12	5	20	8 4
4	8	7	9 4	8	7	14	3 8	12	6	20	10 0
4	9	7	11 0	8	8	14	5 4	12	7	20	11 8
4	10	8	0 8	8	9	14	7 0	12	8	21	1 4
4	11	8	2 4	8	10	14	8 8	12	9	21	3 0
5	0	8	4 0	8	11	14	10 4	12	10	21	4 8
5	1	8	5 8	9	0	15	0 0	12	11	21	6 4
5	2	8	7 4	9	1	15	1 8	13	0	21	8 0
5	3	8	9 0	9	2	15	3 4				
5	4	8	10 8	9	3	15	5 0				

WITH PATENT ACTION.

1-ft. 9-in.

1-ft. 9-in. by			1-ft. 9-in. by			1-ft. 9-in. by		
ft. in.	ft. in.	pts.	ft. in.	ft. in.	pts.	ft. in.	ft. in.	pts.
1 6	= 2 7	6	5 5	= 9 5	9	9 4	=16 4	0
1 7	2 9	3	5 6	9 7	6	9 5	16 5	9
1 8	2 11	0	5 7	9 9	3	9 6	16 7	6
1 9	3 0	9	5 8	9 11	0	9 7	16 9	3
1 10	3 2	6	5 9	10 0	9	9 8	16 11	0
1 11	3 4	3	5 10	10 2	6	9 9	17 0	9
2 0	3 6	0	5 11	10 4	3	9 10	17 2	6
2 1	3 7	9	6 0	10 6	0	9 11	17 4	3
2 2	3 9	6	6 1	10 7	9	10 0	17 6	0
2 3	3 11	3	6 2	10 9	6	10 1	17 7	9
2 4	4 1	0	6 3	10 11	3	10 2	17 9	6
2 5	4 2	9	6 4	11 1	0	10 3	17 11	3
2 6	4 4	6	6 5	11 2	9	10 4	18 1	0
2 7	4 6	3	6 6	11 4	6	10 5	18 2	9
2 8	4 8	0	6 7	11 6	3	10 6	18 4	6
2 9	4 9	9	6 8	11 8	0	10 7	18 6	3
2 10	4 11	6	6 9	11 9	9	10 8	18 8	0
2 11	5 1	3	6 10	11 11	6	10 9	18 9	9
3 0	5 3	0	6 11	12 1	3	10 10	18 11	6
3 1	5 4	9	7 0	12 3	0	10 11	19 1	3
3 2	5 6	6	7 1	12 4	9	11 0	19 3	0
3 3	5 8	3	7 2	12 6	6	11 1	19 4	9
3 4	5 10	0	7 3	12 8	3	11 2	19 6	6
3 5	5 11	9	7 4	12 10	0	11 3	19 8	3
3 6	6 1	6	7 5	12 11	9	11 4	19 10	0
3 7	6 3	3	7 6	13 1	6	11 5	19 11	9
3 8	6 5	0	7 7	13 3	3	11 6	20 1	6
3 9	6 6	9	7 8	13 5	0	11 7	20 3	3
3 10	6 8	6	7 9	13 6	9	11 8	20 5	0
3 11	6 10	3	7 10	13 8	6	11 9	20 6	9
4 0	7 0	0	7 11	13 10	3	11 10	20 8	6
4 1	7 1	9	8 0	14 0	0	11 11	20 10	3
4 2	7 3	6	8 1	14 1	9	12 0	21 0	0
4 3	7 5	3	8 2	14 3	6	12 1	21 1	9
4 4	7 7	0	8 3	14 5	3	12 2	21 3	6
4 5	7 8	9	8 4	14 7	0	12 3	21 5	3
4 6	7 10	6	8 5	14 8	9	12 4	21 7	0
4 7	8 0	3	8 6	14 10	6	12 5	21 8	9
4 8	8 2	0	8 7	15 0	3	12 6	21 10	6
4 9	8 3	9	8 8	15 2	0	12 7	22 0	3
4 10	8 5	6	8 9	15 3	9	12 8	22 2	0
4 11	8 7	3	8 10	15 5	6	12 9	22 3	9
5 0	8 9	0	8 11	15 7	3	12 10	22 5	6
5 1	8 10	9	9 0	15 9	0	12 11	22 7	3
5 2	9 0	6	9 1	15 10	9	13 0	22 9	0
5 3	9 2	3	9 2	16 0	6			
5 4	9 4	0	9 3	16 2	3			

36, FARRINGDON STREET, LONDON, E.C.

SPRING ROLLER BLINDS,

1-ft. 10-in.

1-ft. 10-in. by				1-ft. 10-in. by				1-ft. 10-in. by			
ft. in.	ft.	in.	pts.	ft. in.	ft.	in.	pts.	ft. in.	ft.	iu.	pts.
1 6	= 2	9	0	5 5	= 9	11	2	9 4	=17	1	4
1 7	2	10	10	5 6	10	1	0	9 5	17	3	2
1 8	3	0	8	5 7	10	2	10	9 6	17	5	0
1 9	3	2	6	5 8	10	4	8	9 7	17	6	10
1 10	3	4	4	5 9	10	6	6	9 8	17	8	8
1 11	3	6	2	5 10	10	8	4	9 9	17	10	6
2 0	3	8	0	5 11	10	10	2	9 10	18	0	4
2 1	3	9	10	6 0	11	0	0	9 11	18	2	2
2 2	3	11	8	6 1	11	1	10	10 0	18	4	0
2 3	4	1	6	6 2	11	3	8	10 1	18	5	10
2 4	4	3	4	6 3	11	5	6	10 2	18	7	8
2 5	4	5	2	6 4	11	7	4	10 3	18	9	6
2 6	4	7	0	6 5	11	9	2	10 4	18	11	4
2 7	4	8	10	6 6	11	11	0	10 5	19	1	2
2 8	4	10	8	6 7	12	0	10	10 6	19	3	0
2 9	5	0	6	6 8	12	2	8	10 7	19	4	10
2 10	5	2	4	6 9	12	4	6	10 8	19	6	8
2 11	5	4	2	6 10	12	6	4	10 9	19	8	6
3 0	5	6	0	6 11	12	8	2	10 10	19	10	4
3 1	5	7	10	7 0	12	10	0	10 11	20	0	2
3 2	5	9	8	7 1	12	11	10	11 0	20	2	0
3 3	5	11	6	7 2	13	1	8	11 1	20	3	10
3 4	6	1	4	7 3	13	3	6	11 2	20	5	8
3 5	6	3	2	7 4	13	5	4	11 3	20	7	6
3 6	6	5	0	7 5	13	7	2	11 4	20	9	4
3 7	6	6	10	7 6	13	9	0	11 5	20	11	2
3 8	6	8	8	7 7	13	10	10	11 6	21	1	0
3 9	6	10	6	7 8	14	0	8	11 7	21	2	10
3 10	7	0	4	7 9	14	2	6	11 8	21	4	8
3 11	7	2	2	7 10	14	4	4	11 9	21	6	6
4 0	7	4	0	7 11	14	6	2	11 10	21	8	4
4 1	7	5	10	8 0	14	8	0	11 11	21	10	2
4 2	7	7	8	8 1	14	9	10	12 0	22	0	0
4 3	7	9	6	8 2	14	11	8	12 1	22	1	10
4 4	7	11	4	8 3	15	1	6	12 2	22	3	8
4 5	8	1	2	8 4	15	3	4	12 3	22	5	6
4 6	8	3	0	8 5	15	5	2	12 4	22	7	4
4 7	8	4	10	8 6	15	7	0	12 5	22	9	2
4 8	8	6	8	8 7	15	8	10	12 6	22	11	0
4 9	8	8	6	8 8	15	10	8	12 7	23	0	10
4 10	8	10	4	8 9	16	0	6	12 8	23	2	8
4 11	9	0	2	8 10	16	2	4	12 9	23	4	6
5 0	9	2	0	8 11	16	4	2	12 10	23	6	4
5 1	9	3	10	9 0	16	6	0	12 11	23	8	2
5 2	9	5	8	9 1	16	7	10	13 0	23	10	0
5 3	9	7	6	9 2	16	9	8				
5 4	9	9	4	9 3	16	11	6				

WITH STRIPED HOLLAND.

1-ft. 11-in.

1-ft. 11-in. by			1-ft. 11-in. by			1-ft. 11-in by		
ft. in.	ft. in.	pts.	ft. in.	ft. in.	pts.	ft. in.	ft. in.	pts.
1 6 =	2 10	6	5 5 =	10 4	7	9 4 =	17 10	8
1 7	3 0	5	5 6	10 6	6	9 5	18 0	7
1 8	3 2	4	5 7	10 8	5	9 6	18 2	6
1 9	3 4	3	5 8	10 10	4	9 7	18 4	5
1 10	3 6	2	5 9	11 0	3	9 8	18 6	4
1 11	3 8	1	5 10	11 2	2	9 9	18 8	3
2 0	3 10	0	5 11	11 4	1	9 10	18 10	2
2 1	3 11	11	6 0	11 6	0	9 11	19 0	1
2 2	4 1	10	6 1	11 7	11	10 0	19 2	0
2 3	4 3	9	6 2	11 9	10	10 1	19 3	11
2 4	4 5	8	6 3	11 11	9	10 2	19 5	10
2 5	4 7	7	6 4	12 1	8	10 3	19 7	9
2 6	4 9	6	6 5	12 3	7	10 4	19 9	8
2 7	4 11	5	6 6	12 5	6	10 5	19 11	7
2 8	5 1	4	6 7	12 7	5	10 6	20 1	6
2 9	5 3	3	6 8	12 9	4	10 7	20 3	5
2 10	5 5	2	6 9	12 11	3	10 8	20 5	4
2 11	5 7	1	6 10	13 1	2	10 9	20 7	3
3 0	5 9	0	6 11	13 3	1	10 10	20 9	2
3 1	5 10	11	7 0	13 5	0	10 11	20 11	1
3 2	6 0	10	7 1	13 6	11	11 0	21 1	0
3 3	6 2	9	7 2	13 8	10	11 1	21 2	11
3 4	6 4	8	7 3	13 10	9	11 2	21 4	10
3 5	6 6	7	7 4	14 0	8	11 3	21 6	9
3 6	6 8	6	7 5	14 2	7	11 4	21 8	8
3 7	6 10	5	7 6	14 4	6	11 5	21 10	7
3 8	7 0	4	7 7	14 6	5	11 6	22 0	6
3 9	7 2	3	7 8	14 8	4	11 7	22 2	5
3 10	7 4	2	7 9	14 10	3	11 8	22 4	4
3 11	7 6	1	7 10	15 0	2	11 9	22 6	3
4 0	7 8	0	7 11	15 2	1	11 10	22 8	2
4 1	7 9	11	8 0	15 4	0	11 11	22 10	1
4 2	7 11	10	8 1	15 5	11	12 0	23 0	0
4 3	8 1	9	8 2	15 7	10	12 1	23 1	11
4 4	8 3	8	8 3	15 9	9	12 2	23 3	10
4 5	8 5	7	8 4	15 11	8	12 3	23 5	9
4 6	8 7	6	8 5	16 1	7	12 4	23 7	8
4 7	8 9	5	8 6	16 3	6	12 5	23 9	7
4 8	8 11	4	8 7	16 5	5	12 6	23 11	6
4 9	9 1	3	8 8	16 7	4	12 7	24 1	5
4 10	9 3	2	8 9	16 9	3	12 8	24 3	4
4 11	9 5	1	8 10	16 11	2	12 9	24 5	3
5 0	9 7	0	8 11	17 1	1	12 10	24 7	2
5 1	9 8	11	9 0	17 3	0	12 11	24 9	1
5 2	9 10	10	9 1	17 4	11	13 0	24 11	0
5 3	10 0	9	9 2	17 6	10			
5 4	10 2	8	9 3	17 8	9			

2-ft.

2-ft. by				2-ft. by				2-ft. by		
ft. in.	ft.	in.	pts.	ft. in.	ft.	in.	pts.	ft. in.	ft.	in.	pts.
1 6 =	3	0	0	5 5 =	10	10	0	9 4 =	18	8	0
1 7	3	2	0	5 6	11	0	0	9 5	18	10	0
1 8	3	4	0	5 7	11	2	0	9 6	19	0	0
1 9	3	6	0	5 8	11	4	0	9 7	19	2	0
1 10	3	8	0	5 9	11	6	0	9 8	19	4	0
1 11	3	10	0	5 10	11	8	0	9 9	19	6	0
2 0	4	0	0	5 11	11	10	0	9 10	19	8	0
2 1	4	2	0	6 0	12	0	0	9 11	19	10	0
2 2	4	4	0	6 1	12	2	0	10 0	20	0	0
2 3	4	6	0	6 2	12	4	0	10 1	20	2	0
2 4	4	8	0	6 3	12	6	0	10 2	20	4	0
2 5	4	10	0	6 4	12	8	0	10 3	20	6	0
2 6	5	0	0	6 5	12	10	0	10 4	20	8	0
2 7	5	2	0	6 6	13	0	0	10 5	20	10	0
2 8	5	4	0	6 7	13	2	0	10 6	21	0	0
2 9	5	6	0	6 8	13	4	0	10 7	21	2	0
2 10	5	8	0	6 9	13	6	0	10 8	21	4	0
2 11	5	10	0	6 10	13	8	0	10 9	21	6	0
3 0	6	0	0	6 11	13	10	0	10 10	21	8	0
3 1	6	2	0	7 0	14	0	0	10 11	21	10	0
3 2	6	4	0	7 1	14	2	0	11 0	22	0	0
3 3	6	6	0	7 2	14	4	0	11 1	22	2	0
3 4	6	8	0	7 3	14	6	0	11 2	22	4	0
3 5	6	10	0	7 4	14	8	0	11 3	22	6	0
3 6	7	0	0	7 5	14	10	0	11 4	22	8	0
3 7	7	2	0	7 6	15	0	0	11 5	22	10	0
3 8	7	4	0	7 7	15	2	0	11 6	23	0	0
3 9	7	6	0	7 8	15	4	0	11 7	23	2	0
3 10	7	8	0	7 9	15	6	0	11 8	23	4	0
3 11	7	10	0	7 10	15	8	0	11 9	23	6	0
4 0	8	0	0	7 11	15	10	0	11 10	23	8	0
4 1	8	2	0	8 0	16	0	0	11 11	23	10	0
4 2	8	4	0	8 1	16	2	0	12 0	24	0	0
4 3	8	6	0	8 2	16	4	0	12 1	24	2	0
4 4	8	8	0	8 3	16	6	0	12 2	24	4	0
4 5	8	10	0	8 4	16	8	0	12 3	24	6	0
4 6	9	0	0	8 5	16	10	0	12 4	24	8	0
4 7	9	2	0	8 6	17	0	0	12 5	24	10	0
4 8	9	4	0	8 7	17	2	0	12 6	25	0	0
4 9	9	6	0	8 8	17	4	0	12 7	25	2	0
4 10	9	8	0	8 9	17	6	0	12 8	25	4	0
4 11	9	10	0	8 10	17	8	0	12 9	25	6	0
5 0	10	0	0	8 11	17	10	0	12 10	25	8	0
5 1	10	2	0	9 0	18	0	0	12 11	25	10	0
5 2	10	4	0	9 1	18	2	0	13 0	26	0	0
5 3	10	6	0	9 2	18	4	0				
5 4	10	8	0	9 3	18	6	0				

FOR SCHOOLS AND PUBLIC BUILDINGS.

2-ft. 1-in.

2-ft. 1-in. by				2-ft. 1-in. by				2-ft. 1-in. by			
ft. in.	ft.	in.	pts.	ft. in.	ft.	in.	pts.	ft. in.	ft.	in.	pts.
1 6	= 3	1	6	5 5	=11	3	5	9 4	=19	5	4
1 7	3	3	7	5 6	11	5	6	9 5	19	7	5
1 8	3	5	8	5 7	11	7	7	9 6	19	9	6
1 9	3	7	9	5 8	11	9	8	9 7	19	11	7
1 10	3	9	10	5 9	11	11	9	9 8	20	1	8
1 11	3	11	11	5 10	12	1	10	9 9	20	3	9
2 0	4	2	0	5 11	12	3	11	9 10	20	5	10
2 1	4	4	1	6 0	12	6	0	9 11	20	7	11
2 2	4	6	2	6 1	12	8	1	10 0	20	10	0
2 3	4	8	3	6 2	12	10	2	10 1	21	0	1
2 4	4	10	4	6 3	13	0	3	10 2	21	2	2
2 5	5	0	5	6 4	13	2	4	10 3	21	4	3
2 6	5	2	6	6 5	13	4	5	10 4	21	6	4
2 7	5	4	7	6 6	13	6	6	10 5	21	8	5
2 8	5	6	8	6 7	13	8	7	10 6	21	10	6
2 9	5	8	9	6 8	13	10	8	10 7	22	0	7
2 10	5	10	10	6 9	14	0	9	10 8	22	2	8
2 11	6	0	11	6 10	14	2	10	10 9	22	4	9
3 0	6	3	0	6 11	14	4	11	10 10	22	6	10
3 1	6	5	1	7 0	14	7	0	10 11	22	8	11
3 2	6	7	2	7 1	14	9	1	11 0	22	11	0
3 3	6	9	3	7 2	14	11	2	11 1	23	1	1
3 4	6	11	4	7 3	15	1	3	11 2	23	3	2
3 5	7	1	5	7 4	15	3	4	11 3	23	5	3
3 6	7	3	6	7 5	15	5	5	11 4	23	7	4
3 7	7	5	7	7 6	15	7	6	11 5	23	9	5
3 8	7	7	8	7 7	15	9	7	11 6	23	11	6
3 9	7	9	9	7 8	15	11	8	11 7	24	1	7
3 10	7	11	10	7 9	16	1	9	11 8	24	3	8
3 11	8	1	11	7 10	16	3	10	11 9	24	5	9
4 0	8	4	0	7 11	16	5	11	11 10	24	7	10
4 1	8	6	1	8 0	16	8	0	11 11	24	9	11
4 2	8	8	2	8 1	16	10	1	12 0	25	0	0
4 3	8	10	3	8 2	17	0	2	12 1	25	2	1
4 4	9	0	4	8 3	17	2	3	12 2	25	4	2
4 5	9	2	5	8 4	17	4	4	12 3	25	6	3
4 6	9	4	6	8 5	17	6	5	12 4	25	8	4
4 7	9	6	7	8 6	17	8	6	12 5	25	10	5
4 8	9	8	8	8 7	17	10	7	12 6	26	0	6
4 9	9	10	9	8 8	18	0	8	12 7	26	2	7
4 10	10	0	10	8 9	18	2	9	12 8	26	4	8
4 11	10	2	11	8 10	18	4	10	12 9	26	6	9
5 0	10	5	0	8 11	18	6	11	12 10	26	8	10
5 1	10	7	1	9 0	18	9	0	12 11	26	10	11
5 2	10	9	2	9 1	18	11	1	13 0	27	1	0
5 3	10	11	3	9 2	19	1	2				
5 4	11	1	4	9 3	19	3	3				

2-ft. 2-in.

2-ft. 2-in. by				2-ft. 2-in. by				2-ft. 2-in. by			
ft.	in.	ft.	in. pts.	ft.	in.	ft.	in. pts.	ft.	in.	ft.	in. pts.
1	6	= 3	3 0	5	5	=11	8 10	9	4	=20	2 8
1	7	3	5 2	5	6	11	11 0	9	5	20	4 10
1	8	3	7 4	5	7	12	1 2	9	6	20	7 0
1	9	3	9 6	5	8	12	3 4	9	7	20	9 2
1	10	3	11 8	5	9	12	5 6	9	8	20	11 4
1	11	4	1 10	5	10	12	7 8	9	9	21	1 6
2	0	4	4 0	5	11	12	9 10	9	10	21	3 8
2	1	4	6 2	6	0	13	0 0	9	11	21	5 10
2	2	4	8 4	6	1	13	2 2	10	0	21	8 0
2	3	4	10 6	6	2	13	4 4	10	1	21	10 2
2	4	5	0 8	6	3	13	6 6	10	2	22	0 4
2	5	5	2 10	6	4	13	8 8	10	3	22	2 6
2	6	5	5 0	6	5	13	10 10	10	4	22	4 8
2	7	5	7 2	6	6	14	1 0	10	5	22	6 10
2	8	5	9 4	6	7	14	3 2	10	6	22	9 0
2	9	5	11 6	6	8	14	5 4	10	7	22	11 2
2	10	6	1 8	6	9	14	7 6	10	8	23	1 4
2	11	6	3 10	6	10	14	9 8	10	9	23	3 6
3	0	6	6 0	6	11	14	11 10	10	10	23	5 8
3	1	6	8 2	7	0	15	2 0	10	11	23	7 10
3	2	6	10 4	7	1	15	4 2	11	0	23	10 0
3	3	7	0 6	7	2	15	6 4	11	1	24	0 2
3	4	7	2 8	7	3	15	8 6	11	2	24	2 4
3	5	7	4 10	7	4	15	10 8	11	3	24	4 6
3	6	7	7 0	7	5	16	0 10	11	4	24	6 8
3	7	7	9 2	7	6	16	3 0	11	5	24	8 10
3	8	7	11 4	7	7	16	5 2	11	6	24	11 0
3	9	8	1 6	7	8	16	7 4	11	7	25	1 2
3	10	8	3 8	7	9	16	9 6	11	8	25	3 4
3	11	8	5 10	7	10	16	11 8	11	9	25	5 6
4	0	8	8 0	7	11	17	1 10	11	10	25	7 8
4	1	8	10 2	8	0	17	4 0	11	11	25	9 10
4	2	9	0 4	8	1	17	6 2	12	0	26	0 0
4	3	9	2 6	8	2	17	8 4	12	1	26	2 2
4	4	9	4 8	8	3	17	10 6	12	2	26	4 4
4	5	9	6 10	8	4	18	0 8	12	3	26	6 6
4	6	9	9 0	8	5	18	2 10	12	4	26	8 8
4	7	9	11 2	8	6	18	5 0	12	5	26	10 10
4	8	10	1 4	8	7	18	7 2	12	6	27	1 0
4	9	10	3 6	8	8	18	9 4	12	7	27	3 2
4	10	10	5 8	8	9	18	11 6	12	8	27	5 4
4	11	10	7 10	8	10	19	1 8	12	9	27	7 6
5	0	10	10 0	8	11	19	3 10	12	10	27	9 8
5	1	11	0 2	9	0	19	6 0	12	11	27	11 10
5	2	11	2 4	9	1	19	8 2	13	0	28	2 0
5	3	11	4 6	9	2	19	10 4				
5	4	11	6 8	9	3	20	0 6				

OF SILK OR MUSLIN.

2-ft. 3-in.

ft. in.	ft. in. pts.	ft. in.	ft. in. pts.	ft. in.	ft. in. pts.
2-ft. 3-in. by		**2-ft. 3-in. by**		**2-ft. 3-in. by**	
1 6	= 3 4 6	5 5	=12 2 3	9 4	=21 0 0
1 7	3 6 9	5 6	12 4 6	9 5	21 2 3
1 8	3 9 0	5 7	12 6 9	9 6	21 4 6
1 9	3 11 3	5 8	12 9 0	9 7	21 6 9
1 10	4 1 6	5 9	12 11 3	9 8	21 9 0
1 11	4 3 9	5 10	13 1 6	9 9	21 11 3
2 0	4 6 0	5 11	13 3 9	9 10	22 1 6
2 1	4 8 3	6 0	13 6 0	9 11	22 3 9
2 2	4 10 6	6 1	13 8 3	10 0	22 6 0
2 3	5 0 9	6 2	13 10 6	10 1	22 8 3
2 4	5 3 0	6 3	14 0 9	10 2	22 10 6
2 5	5 5 3	6 4	14 3 0	10 3	23 0 9
2 6	5 7 6	6 5	14 5 3	10 4	23 3 0
2 7	5 9 9	6 6	14 7 6	10 5	23 5 3
2 8	6 0 0	6 7	14 9 9	10 6	23 7 6
2 9	6 2 3	6 8	15 0 0	10 7	23 9 9
2 10	6 4 6	6 9	15 2 3	10 8	24 0 0
2 11	6 6 9	6 10	15 4 6	10 9	24 2 3
3 0	6 9 0	6 11	15 6 9	10 10	24 4 6
3 1	6 11 3	7 0	15 9 0	10 11	24 6 9
3 2	7 1 6	7 1	15 11 3	11 0	24 9 0
3 3	7 3 9	7 2	16 1 6	11 1	24 11 3
3 4	7 6 0	7 3	16 3 9	11 2	25 1 6
3 5	7 8 3	7 4	16 6 0	11 3	25 3 9
3 6	7 10 6	7 5	16 8 3	11 4	25 6 0
3 7	8 0 9	7 6	16 10 6	11 5	25 8 3
3 8	8 3 0	7 7	17 0 9	11 6	25 10 6
3 9	8 5 3	7 8	17 3 0	11 7	26 0 9
3 10	8 7 6	7 9	17 5 3	11 8	26 3 0
3 11	8 9 9	7 10	17 7 6	11 9	26 5 3
4 0	9 0 0	7 11	17 9 9	11 10	26 7 6
4 1	9 2 3	8 0	18 0 0	11 11	26 9 9
4 2	9 4 6	8 1	18 2 3	12 0	27 0 0
4 3	9 6 9	8 2	18 4 6	12 1	27 2 3
4 4	9 9 0	8 3	18 6 9	12 2	27 4 6
4 5	9 11 3	8 4	18 9 0	12 3	27 6 9
4 6	10 1 6	8 5	18 11 3	12 4	27 9 0
4 7	10 3 9	8 6	19 1 6	12 5	27 11 3
4 8	10 6 0	8 7	19 3 9	12 6	28 1 6
4 9	10 8 3	8 8	19 6 0	12 7	28 3 9
4 10	10 10 6	8 9	19 8 3	12 8	28 6 0
4 11	11 0 9	8 10	19 10 6	12 9	28 8 3
5 0	11 3 0	8 11	20 0 9	12 10	28 10 6
5 1	11 5 3	9 0	20 3 0	12 11	29 0 9
5 2	11 7 6	9 1	20 5 3	13 0	29 3 0
5 3	11 9 9	9 2	20 7 6		
5 4	12 0 0	9 3	20 9 9		

36, FARRINGDON STREET, LONDON, E.C.

2-ft. 4-in.

2-ft. 4-in. by				2-ft. 4-in. by				2-ft. 4-in. by			
ft. in.		ft. in. pts.		ft. in.		ft. in. pts.		ft. in.		ft. in. pts.	
1	6	= 3	6	0	5	5	=12	7	8	9	4	=21	9	4
1	7	3	8	4	5	6	12	10	0	9	5	21	11	8
1	8	3	10	8	5	7	13	0	4	9	6	22	2	0
1	9	4	1	0	5	8	13	2	8	9	7	22	4	4
1	10	4	3	4	5	9	13	5	0	9	8	22	6	8
1	11	4	5	8	5	10	13	7	4	9	9	22	9	0
2	0	4	8	0	5	11	13	9	8	9	10	22	11	4
2	1	4	10	4	6	0	14	0	0	9	11	23	1	8
2	2	5	0	8	6	1	14	2	4	10	0	23	4	0
2	3	5	3	0	6	2	14	4	8	10	1	23	6	4
2	4	5	5	4	6	3	14	7	0	10	2	23	8	8
2	5	5	7	8	6	4	14	9	4	10	3	23	11	0
2	6	5	10	0	6	5	14	11	8	10	4	24	1	4
2	7	6	0	4	6	6	15	2	0	10	5	24	3	8
2	8	6	2	8	6	7	15	4	4	10	6	24	6	0
2	9	6	5	0	6	8	15	6	8	10	7	24	8	4
2	10	6	7	4	6	9	15	9	0	10	8	24	10	8
2	11	6	9	8	6	10	15	11	4	10	9	25	1	0
3	0	7	0	0	6	11	16	1	8	10	10	25	3	4
3	1	7	2	4	7	0	16	4	0	10	11	25	5	8
3	2	7	4	8	7	1	16	6	4	11	0	25	8	0
3	3	7	7	0	7	2	16	8	8	11	1	25	10	4
3	4	7	9	4	7	3	16	11	0	11	2	26	0	8
3	5	7	11	8	7	4	17	1	4	11	3	26	3	0
3	6	8	2	0	7	5	17	3	8	11	4	26	5	4
3	7	8	4	4	7	6	17	6	0	11	5	26	7	8
3	8	8	6	8	7	7	17	8	4	11	6	26	10	0
3	9	8	9	0	7	8	17	10	8	11	7	27	0	4
3	10	8	11	4	7	9	18	1	0	11	8	27	2	8
3	11	9	1	8	7	10	18	3	4	11	9	27	5	0
4	0	9	4	0	7	11	18	5	8	11	10	27	7	4
4	1	9	6	4	8	0	18	8	0	11	11	27	9	8
4	2	9	8	8	8	1	18	10	4	12	0	28	0	0
4	3	9	11	0	8	2	19	0	8	12	1	28	2	4
4	4	10	1	4	8	3	19	3	0	12	2	28	4	8
4	5	10	3	8	8	4	19	5	4	12	3	28	7	0
4	6	10	6	0	8	5	19	7	8	12	4	28	9	4
4	7	10	8	4	8	6	19	10	0	12	5	28	11	8
4	8	10	10	8	8	7	20	0	4	12	6	29	2	0
4	9	11	1	0	8	8	20	2	8	12	7	29	4	4
4	10	11	3	4	8	9	20	5	0	12	8	29	6	8
4	11	11	5	8	8	10	20	7	4	12	9	29	9	0
5	0	11	8	0	8	11	20	9	8	12	10	29	11	4
5	1	11	10	4	9	0	21	0	0	12	11	30	1	8
5	2	12	0	8	9	1	21	2	4	13	0	30	4	0
5	3	12	3	0	9	2	21	4	8					
5	4	12	5	4	9	3	21	7	0					

WITH METAL TUBE TOP RAILS.

2-ft. 5-in.

2-ft. 5-in. by			2-ft. 5-in. by			2-ft. 5-in. by		
ft. in.	ft. in. pts.		ft. in.	ft. in. pts.		ft. in.	ft. in. pts.	
1 6	= 3 7 6		5 5	=13 1 1		9 4	=22 6 8	
1 7	3 9 11		5 6	13 3 6		9 5	22 9 1	
1 8	4 0 4		5 7	13 5 11		9 6	22 11 6	
1 9	4 2 9		5 8	13 8 4		9 7	23 1 11	
1 10	4 5 2		5 9	13 10 9		9 8	23 4 4	
1 11	4 7 7		5 10	14 1 2		9 9	23 6 9	
2 0	4 10 0		5 11	14 3 7		9 10	23 9 2	
2 1	5 0 5		6 0	14 6 0		9 11	23 11 7	
2 2	5 2 10		6 1	14 8 5		10 0	24 2 0	
2 3	5 5 3		6 2	14 10 10		10 1	24 4 5	
2 4	5 7 8		6 3	15 1 3		10 2	24 6 10	
2 5	5 10 1		6 4	15 3 8		10 3	24 9 3	
2 6	6 0 6		6 5	15 6 1		10 4	24 11 8	
2 7	6 2 11		6 6	15 8 6		10 5	25 2 1	
2 8	6 5 4		6 7	15 10 11		10 6	25 4 6	
2 9	6 7 9		6 8	16 1 4		10 7	25 6 11	
2 10	6 10 2		6 9	16 3 9		10 8	25 9 4	
2 11	7 0 7		6 10	16 6 2		10 9	25 11 9	
3 0	7 3 0		6 11	16 8 7		10 10	26 2 2	
3 1	7 5 5		7 0	16 11 0		10 11	26 4 7	
3 2	7 7 10		7 1	17 1 5		11 0	26 7 0	
3 3	7 10 3		7 2	17 3 10		11 1	26 9 5	
3 4	8 0 8		7 3	17 6 3		11 2	26 11 10	
3 5	8 3 1		7 4	17 8 8		11 3	27 2 3	
3 6	8 5 6		7 5	17 11 1		11 4	27 4 8	
3 7	8 7 11		7 6	18 1 6		11 5	27 7 1	
3 8	8 10 4		7 7	18 3 11		11 6	27 9 6	
3 9	9 0 9		7 8	18 6 4		11 7	27 11 11	
3 10	9 3 2		7 9	18 8 9		11 8	28 2 4	
3 11	9 5 7		7 10	18 11 2		11 9	28 4 9	
4 0	9 8 0		7 11	19 1 7		11 10	28 7 2	
4 1	9 10 5		8 0	19 4 0		11 11	28 9 7	
4 2	10 0 10		8 1	19 6 5		12 0	29 0 0	
4 3	10 3 3		8 2	19 8 10		12 1	29 2 5	
4 4	10 5 8		8 3	19 11 3		12 2	29 4 10	
4 5	10 8 1		8 4	20 1 8		12 3	29 7 3	
4 6	10 10 6		8 5	20 4 1		12 4	29 9 8	
4 7	11 0 11		8 6	20 6 6		12 5	30 0 1	
4 8	11 3 4		8 7	20 8 11		12 6	30 2 6	
4 9	11 5 9		8 8	20 11 4		12 7	30 4 11	
4 10	11 8 2		8 9	21 1 9		12 8	30 7 4	
4 11	11 10 7		8 10	21 4 2		12 9	30 9 9	
5 0	12 1 0		8 11	21 6 7		12 10	31 0 2	
5 1	12 3 5		9 0	21 9 0		12 11	31 2 7	
5 2	12 5 10		9 1	21 11 5		13 0	31 5 0	
5 3	12 8 3		9 2	22 1 10				
5 4	12 10 8		9 3	22 4 3				

FLORENTINE BLINDS,

2-ft. 6-in.

2-ft. 6-in. by			2-ft. 6-in. by			2-ft. 6-in. by		
ft. in.	ft. in.	pts.	ft. in.	ft. in.	pts.	ft. in.	ft. in.	pts.
1 6	= 3 9	0	5 5	=13 6	6	9 4	=23 4	0
1 7	3 11	6	5 6	13 9	0	9 5	23 6	6
1 8	4 2	0	5 7	13 11	6	9 6	23 9	0
1 9	4 4	6	5 8	14 2	0	9 7	23 11	6
1 10	4 7	0	5 9	14 4	6	9 8	24 2	0
1 11	4 9	6	5 10	14 7	0	9 9	24 4	6
2 0	5 0	0	5 11	14 9	6	9 10	24 7	0
2 1	5 2	6	6 0	15 0	0	9 11	24 9	6
2 2	5 5	0	6 1	15 2	6	10 0	25 0	0
2 3	5 7	6	6 2	15 5	0	10 1	25 2	6
2 4	5 10	0	6 3	15 7	6	10 2	25 5	0
2 5	6 0	6	6 4	15 10	0	10 3	25 7	6
2 6	6 3	0	6 5	16 0	6	10 4	25 10	0
2 7	6 5	6	6 6	16 3	0	10 5	26 0	6
2 8	6 8	0	6 7	16 5	6	10 6	26 3	0
2 9	6 10	6	6 8	16 8	0	10 7	26 5	6
2 10	7 1	0	6 9	16 10	6	10 8	26 8	0
2 11	7 3	6	6 10	17 1	0	10 9	26 10	6
3 0	7 6	0	6 11	17 3	6	10 10	27 1	0
3 1	7 8	6	7 0	17 6	0	10 11	27 3	6
3 2	7 11	0	7 1	17 8	6	11 0	27 6	0
3 3	8 1	6	7 2	17 11	0	11 1	27 8	6
3 4	8 4	0	7 3	18 1	6	11 2	27 11	0
3 5	8 6	6	7 4	18 4	0	11 3	28 1	6
3 6	8 9	0	7 5	18 6	6	11 4	28 4	0
3 7	8 11	6	7 6	18 9	0	11 5	28 6	6
3 8	9 2	0	7 7	18 11	6	11 6	28 9	0
3 9	9 4	6	7 8	19 2	0	11 7	28 11	6
3 10	9 7	0	7 9	19 4	6	11 8	29 2	0
3 11	9 9	6	7 10	19 7	0	11 9	29 4	6
4 0	10 0	0	7 11	19 9	6	11 10	29 7	0
4 1	10 2	6	8 0	20 0	0	11 11	29 9	6
4 2	10 5	0	8 1	20 2	6	12 0	30 0	0
4 3	10 7	6	8 2	20 5	0	12 1	30 2	6
4 4	10 10	0	8 3	20 7	6	12 2	30 5	0
4 5	11 0	6	8 4	20 10	0	12 3	30 7	6
4 6	11 3	0	8 5	21 0	6	12 4	30 10	0
4 7	11 5	6	8 6	21 3	0	12 5	31 0	6
4 8	11 8	0	8 7	21 5	6	12 6	31 3	0
4 9	11 10	6	8 8	21 8	0	12 7	31 5	6
4 10	12 1	0	8 9	21 10	6	12 8	31 8	0
4 11	12 3	6	8 10	22 1	0	12 9	31 10	6
5 0	12 6	0	8 11	22 3	6	12 10	32 1	0
5 1	12 8	6	9 0	22 6	0	12 11	32 3	6
5 2	12 11	0	9 1	22 8	6	13 0	32 6	0
5 3	13 1	6	9 2	22 11	0			
5 4	13 4	0	9 3	23 1	6			

FOR CASEMENT WINDOWS.

2

2-ft. 7-in.

2-ft. 7-in. by			2-ft. 7-in. by			2-ft. 7-in. by		
ft. in.	ft. in.	pts.	ft. in.	ft. in.	pts.	ft. in.	ft. in.	pts.
1 6	= 3 10	6	5 5	=13 11	11	9 4	=24 1	4
1 7	4 1	1	5 6	14 2	6	9 5	24 3	11
1 8	4 3	8	5 7	14 5	1	9 6	24 6	6
1 9	4 6	3	5 8	14 7	8	9 7	24 9	1
1 10	4 8	10	5 9	14 10	3	9 8	24 11	8
1 11	4 11	5	5 10	15 0	10	9 9	25 2	3
2 0	5 2	0	5 11	15 3	5	9 10	25 4	10
2 1	5 4	7	6 0	15 6	0	9 11	25 7	5
2 2	5 7	2	6 1	15 8	7	10 0	25 10	0
2 3	5 9	9	6 2	15 11	2	10 1	26 0	7
2 4	6 0	4	6 3	16 1	9	10 2	26 3	2
2 5	6 2	11	6 4	16 4	4	10 3	26 5	9
2 6	6 5	6	6 5	16 6	11	10 4	26 8	4
2 7	6 8	1	6 6	16 9	6	10 5	26 10	11
2 8	6 10	8	6 7	17 0	1	10 6	27 1	6
2 9	7 1	3	6 8	17 2	8	10 7	27 4	1
2 10	7 3	10	6 9	17 5	3	10 8	27 6	8
2 11	7 6	5	6 10	17 7	10	10 9	27 9	3
3 0	7 9	0	6 11	17 10	5	10 10	27 11	10
3 1	7 11	7	7 0	18 1	0	10 11	28 2	5
3 2	8 2	2	7 1	18 3	7	11 0	28 5	0
3 3	8 4	9	7 2	18 6	2	11 1	28 7	7
3 4	8 7	4	7 3	18 8	9	11 2	28 10	2
3 5	8 9	11	7 4	18 11	4	11 3	29 0	9
3 6	9 0	6	7 5	19 1	11	11 4	29 3	4
3 7	9 3	1	7 6	19 4	6	11 5	29 5	11
3 8	9 5	8	7 7	19 7	1	11 6	29 8	6
3 9	9 8	3	7 8	19 9	8	11 7	29 11	1
3 10	9 10	10	7 9	20 0	3	11 8	30 1	8
3 11	10 1	5	7 10	20 2	10	11 9	30 4	3
4 0	10 4	0	7 11	20 5	5	11 10	30 6	10
4 1	10 6	7	8 0	20 8	0	11 11	30 9	5
4 2	10 9	2	8 1	20 10	7	12 0	31 0	0
4 3	10 11	9	8 2	21 1	2	12 1	31 2	7
4 4	11 2	4	8 3	21 3	9	12 2	31 5	2
4 5	11 4	11	8 4	21 6	4	12 3	31 7	9
4 6	11 7	6	8 5	21 8	11	12 4	31 10	4
4 7	11 10	1	8 6	21 11	6	12 5	32 0	11
4 8	12 0	8	8 7	22 2	1	12 6	32 3	6
4 9	12 3	3	8 8	22 4	8	12 7	32 6	1
4 10	12 5	10	8 9	22 7	3	12 8	32 8	8
4 11	12 8	5	8 10	22 9	10	12 9	32 11	3
5 0	12 11	0	8 11	23 0	5	12 10	33 1	10
5 1	13 1	7	9 0	23 3	0	12 11	33 4	5
5 2	13 4	2	9 1	23 5	7	13 0	33 7	0
5 3	13 6	9	9 2	23 8	2			
5 4	13 9	4	9 3	23 10	9			

2-ft. 8-in.

2-ft. 8-in. by			2-ft. 8-in. by			2-ft. 8-in. by		
ft. in.	ft. in. pts.		ft. in.	ft. in. pts.		ft. in.	ft. in. pts.	
1 6	= 4 0 0		5 5	=14 5 4		9 4	=24 10 8	
1 7	4 2 8		5 6	14 8 0		9 5	25 1 4	
1 8	4 5 4		5 7	14 10 8		9 6	25 4 0	
1 9	4 8 0		5 8	15 1 4		9 7	25 6 8	
1 10	4 10 8		5 9	15 4 0		9 8	25 9 4	
1 11	5 1 4		5 10	15 6 8		9 9	26 0 0	
2 0	5 4 0		5 11	15 9 4		9 10	26 2 8	
2 1	5 6 8		6 0	16 0 0		9 11	26 5 4	
2 2	5 9 4		6 1	16 2 8		10 0	26 8 0	
2 3	6 0 0		6 2	16 5 4		10 1	26 10 8	
2 4	6 2 8		6 3	16 8 0		10 2	27 1 4	
2 5	6 5 4		6 4	16 10 8		10 3	27 4 0	
2 6	6 8 0		6 5	17 1 4		10 4	27 6 8	
2 7	6 10 8		6 6	17 4 0		10 5	27 9 4	
2 8	7 1 4		6 7	17 6 8		10 6	28 0 0	
2 9	7 4 0		6 8	17 9 4		10 7	28 2 8	
2 10	7 6 8		6 9	18 0 0		10 8	28 5 4	
2 11	7 9 4		6 10	18 2 8		10 9	28 8 0	
3 0	8 0 0		6 11	18 5 4		10 10	28 10 8	
3 1	8 2 8		7 0	18 8 0		10 11	29 1 4	
3 2	8 5 4		7 1	18 10 8		11 0	29 4 0	
3 3	8 8 0		7 2	19 1 4		11 1	29 6 8	
3 4	8 10 8		7 3	19 4 0		11 2	29 9 4	
3 5	9 1 4		7 4	19 6 8		11 3	30 0 0	
3 6	9 4 0		7 5	19 9 4		11 4	30 2 8	
3 7	9 6 8		7 6	20 0 0		11 5	30 5 4	
3 8	9 9 4		7 7	20 2 8		11 6	30 8 0	
3 9	10 0 0		7 8	20 5 4		11 7	30 10 8	
3 10	10 2 8		7 9	20 8 0		11 8	31 1 4	
3 11	10 5 4		7 10	20 10 8		11 9	31 4 0	
4 0	10 8 0		7 11	21 1 4		11 10	31 6 8	
4 1	10 10 8		8 0	21 4 0		11 11	31 9 4	
4 2	11 1 4		8 1	21 6 8		12 0	32 0 0	
4 3	11 4 0		8 2	21 9 4		12 1	32 2 8	
4 4	11 6 8		8 3	22 0 0		12 2	32 5 4	
4 5	11 9 4		8 4	22 2 8		12 3	32 8 0	
4 6	12 0 0		8 5	22 5 4		12 4	32 10 8	
4 7	12 2 8		8 6	22 8 0		12 5	33 1 4	
4 8	12 5 4		8 7	22 10 8		12 6	33 4 0	
4 9	12 8 0		8 8	23 1 4		12 7	33 6 8	
4 10	12 10 8		8 9	23 4 0		12 8	33 9 4	
4 11	13 1 4		8 10	23 6 8		12 9	34 0 0	
5 0	13 4 0		8 11	23 9 4		12 10	34 2 8	
5 1	13 6 8		9 0	24 0 0		12 11	34 5 4	
5 2	13 9 4		9 1	24 2 8		13 0	34 8 0	
5 3	14 0 0		9 2	24 5 4				
5 4	14 2 8		9 3	24 8 0				

WITH METAL TUBE SLIDES.

2-ft. 9-in.

2-ft. 9-in. by			2-ft. 9-in. by			2-ft. 9-in. by		
ft. in.	ft. in.	pts.	ft. in.	ft. in.	pts.	ft. in.	ft. in.	pts.
1 6 =	4 1	6	5 5 =	14 10	9	9 4 =	25 8	0
1 7	4 4	3	5 6	15 1	6	9 5	25 10	9
1 8	4 7	0	5 7	15 4	3	9 6	26 1	6
1 9	4 9	9	5 8	15 7	0	9 7	26 4	3
1 10	5 0	6	5 9	15 9	9	9 8	26 7	0
1 11	5 3	3	5 10	16 0	6	9 9	26 9	9
2 0	5 6	0	5 11	16 3	3	9 10	27 0	6
2 1	5 8	9	6 0	16 6	0	9 11	27 3	3
2 2	5 11	6	6 1	16 8	9	10 0	27 6	0
2 3	6 2	3	6 2	16 11	6	10 1	27 8	9
2 4	6 5	0	6 3	17 2	3	10 2	27 11	6
2 5	6 7	9	6 4	17 5	0	10 3	28 2	3
2 6	6 10	6	6 5	17 7	9	10 4	28 5	0
2 7	7 1	3	6 6	17 10	6	10 5	28 7	9
2 8	7 4	0	6 7	18 1	3	10 6	28 10	6
2 9	7 6	9	6 8	18 4	0	10 7	29 1	3
2 10	7 9	6	6 9	18 6	9	10 8	29 4	0
2 11	8 0	3	6 10	18 9	6	10 9	29 6	9
3 0	8 3	0	6 11	19 0	3	10 10	29 9	6
3 1	8 5	9	7 0	19 3	0	10 11	30 0	3
3 2	8 8	6	7 1	19 5	9	11 0	30 3	0
3 3	8 11	3	7 2	19 8	6	11 1	30 5	9
3 4	9 2	0	7 3	19 11	3	11 2	30 8	6
3 5	9 4	9	7 4	20 2	0	11 3	30 11	3
3 6	9 7	6	7 5	20 4	9	11 4	31 2	0
3 7	9 10	3	7 6	20 7	6	11 5	31 4	9
3 8	10 1	0	7 7	20 10	3	11 6	31 7	6
3 9	10 3	9	7 8	21 1	0	11 7	31 10	3
3 10	10 6	6	7 9	21 3	9	11 8	32 1	0
3 11	10 9	3	7 10	21 6	6	11 9	32 3	9
4 0	11 0	0	7 11	21 9	3	11 10	32 6	6
4 1	11 2	9	8 0	22 0	0	11 11	32 9	3
4 2	11 5	6	8 1	22 2	9	12 0	33 0	0
4 3	11 8	3	8 2	22 5	6	12 1	33 2	9
4 4	11 11	0	8 3	22 8	3	12 2	33 5	6
4 5	12 1	9	8 4	22 11	0	12 3	33 8	3
4 6	12 4	6	8 5	23 1	9	12 4	33 11	0
4 7	12 7	3	8 6	23 4	6	12 5	34 1	9
4 8	12 10	0	8 7	23 7	3	12 6	34 4	6
4 9	13 0	9	8 8	23 10	0	12 7	34 7	3
4 10	13 3	6	8 9	24 0	9	12 8	34 10	0
4 11	13 6	3	8 10	24 3	6	12 9	35 0	9
5 0	13 9	0	8 11	24 6	3	12 10	35 3	6
5 1	13 11	9	9 0	24 9	0	12 11	35 6	3
5 2	14 2	6	9 1	24 11	9	13 0	35 9	0
5 3	14 5	3	9 2	25 2	6			
5 4	14 8	0	9 3	25 5	3			

2-ft. 10-in.

2-ft. 10-in. by				2-ft. 10-in. by				2-ft. 10-in. by		
ft.	in.	ft.	in. pts.	ft.	in.	ft.	in. pts.	ft.	in.	ft.	in. pts.
1	6	= 4	3 0	5	5	=15	4 2	9	4	=26	5 4
1	7	4	5 10	5	6	15	7 0	9	5	26	8 2
1	8	4	8 8	5	7	15	9 10	9	6	26	11 0
1	9	4	11 6	5	8	16	0 8	9	7	27	1 10
1	10	5	2 4	5	9	16	3 6	9	8	27	4 8
1	11	5	5 2	5	10	16	6 4	9	9	27	7 6
2	0	5	8 0	5	11	16	9 2	9	10	27	10 4
2	1	5	10 10	6	0	17	0 0	9	11	28	1 2
2	2	6	1 8	6	1	17	2 10	10	0	28	4 0
2	3	6	4 6	6	2	17	5 8	10	1	28	6 10
2	4	6	7 4	6	3	17	8 6	10	2	28	9 8
2	5	6	10 2	6	4	17	11 4	10	3	29	0 6
2	6	7	1 0	6	5	18	2 2	10	4	29	3 4
2	7	7	3 10	6	6	18	5 0	10	5	29	6 2
2	8	7	6 8	6	7	18	7 10	10	6	29	9 0
2	9	7	9 6	6	8	18	10 8	10	7	29	11 10
2	10	8	0 4	6	9	19	1 6	10	8	30	2 8
2	11	8	3 2	6	10	19	4 4	10	9	30	5 6
3	0	8	6 0	6	11	19	7 2	10	10	30	8 4
3	1	8	8 10	7	0	19	10 0	10	11	30	11 2
3	2	8	11 8	7	1	20	0 10	11	0	31	2 0
3	3	9	2 6	7	2	20	3 8	11	1	31	4 10
3	4	9	5 4	7	3	20	6 6	11	2	31	7 8
3	5	9	8 2	7	4	20	9 4	11	3	31	10 6
3	6	9	11 0	7	5	21	0 2	11	4	32	1 4
3	7	10	1 10	7	6	21	3 0	11	5	32	4 2
3	8	10	4 8	7	7	21	5 10	11	6	32	7 0
3	9	10	7 6	7	8	21	8 8	11	7	32	9 10
3	10	10	10 4	7	9	21	11 6	11	8	33	0 8
3	11	11	1 2	7	10	22	2 4	11	9	33	3 6
4	0	11	4 0	7	11	22	5 2	11	10	33	6 4
4	1	11	6 10	8	0	22	8 0	11	11	33	9 2
4	2	11	9 8	8	1	22	10 10	12	0	34	0 0
4	3	12	0 6	8	2	23	1 8	12	1	34	2 10
4	4	12	3 4	8	3	23	4 6	12	2	34	5 8
4	5	12	6 2	8	4	23	7 4	12	3	34	8 6
4	6	12	9 0	8	5	23	10 2	12	4	34	11 4
4	7	12	11 10	8	6	24	1 0	12	5	35	2 2
4	8	13	2 8	8	7	24	3 10	12	6	35	5 0
4	9	13	5 6	8	8	24	6 8	12	7	35	7 10
4	10	13	8 4	8	9	24	9 6	12	8	35	10 8
4	11	13	11 2	8	10	25	0 4	12	9	36	1 6
5	0	14	2 0	8	11	25	3 2	12	10	36	4 4
5	1	14	4 10	9	0	25	6 0	12	11	36	7 2
5	2	14	7 8	9	1	25	8 10	13	0	36	10 0
5	3	14	10 6	9	2	25	11 8				
5	4	15	1 4	9	3	26	2 6				

2-ft. 11-in.

2-ft. 11-in. by				2-ft. 11-in. by				2-ft. 11-in. by			
ft.	in.	ft.	in. pts.	ft.	in.	ft.	in. pts.	ft.	in.	ft.	in. pts.
1	6	= 4	4 6	5	5	=15	9 7	9	4	=27	2 8
1	7	4	7 5	5	6	16	0 6	9	5	27	5 7
1	8	4	10 4	5	7	16	3 5	9	6	27	8 6
1	9	5	1 3	5	8	16	6 4	9	7	27	11 5
1	10	5	4 2	5	9	16	9 3	9	8	28	2 4
1	11	5	7 1	5	10	17	0 2	9	9	28	5 3
2	0	5	10 0	5	11	17	3 1	9	10	28	8 2
2	1	6	0 11	6	0	17	6 0	9	11	28	11 1
2	2	6	3 10	6	1	17	8 11	10	0	29	2 0
2	3	6	6 9	6	2	17	11 10	10	1	29	4 11
2	4	6	9 8	6	3	18	2 9	10	2	29	7 10
2	5	7	0 7	6	4	18	5 8	10	3	29	10 9
2	6	7	3 6	6	5	18	8 7	10	4	30	1 8
2	7	7	6 5	6	6	18	11 6	10	5	30	4 7
2	8	7	9 4	6	7	19	2 5	10	6	30	7 6
2	9	8	0 3	6	8	19	5 4	10	7	30	10 5
2	10	8	3 2	6	9	19	8 3	10	8	31	1 4
2	11	8	6 1	6	10	19	11 2	10	9	31	4 3
3	0	8	9 0	6	11	20	2 1	10	10	31	7 2
3	1	8	11 11	7	0	20	5 0	10	11	31	10 1
3	2	9	2 10	7	1	20	7 11	11	0	32	1 0
3	3	9	5 9	7	2	20	10 10	11	1	32	3 11
3	4	9	8 8	7	3	21	1 9	11	2	32	6 10
3	5	9	11 7	7	4	21	4 8	11	3	32	9 9
3	6	10	2 6	7	5	21	7 7	11	4	33	0 8
3	7	10	5 5	7	6	21	10 6	11	5	33	3 7
3	8	10	8 4	7	7	22	1 5	11	6	33	6 6
3	9	10	11 3	7	8	22	4 4	11	7	33	9 5
3	10	11	2 2	7	9	22	7 3	11	8	34	0 4
3	11	11	5 1	7	10	22	10 2	11	9	34	3 3
4	0	11	8 0	7	11	23	1 1	11	10	34	6 2
4	1	11	10 11	8	0	23	4 0	11	11	34	9 1
4	2	12	1 10	8	1	23	6 11	12	0	35	0 0
4	3	12	4 9	8	2	23	9 10	12	1	35	2 11
4	4	12	7 8	8	3	24	0 9	12	2	35	5 10
4	5	12	10 7	8	4	24	3 8	12	3	35	8 9
4	6	13	1 6	8	5	24	6 7	12	4	35	11 8
4	7	13	4 5	8	6	24	9 6	12	5	36	2 7
4	8	13	7 4	8	7	25	0 5	12	6	36	5 6
4	9	13	10 3	8	8	25	3 4	12	7	36	8 5
4	10	14	1 2	8	9	25	6 3	12	8	36	11 4
4	11	14	4 1	8	10	25	9 2	12	9	37	2 3
5	0	14	7 0	8	11	26	0 1	12	10	37	5 2
5	1	14	9 11	9	0	26	3 0	12	11	37	8 1
5	2	15	0 10	9	1	26	5 11	13	0	37	11 0
5	3	15	3 9	9	2	26	8 10				
5	4	15	6 8	9	3	26	11 9				

3-ft.

3-ft. by

ft. in.	ft. in. pts.
1 6	= 4 6 0
1 7	4 9 0
1 8	5 0 0
1 9	5 3 0
1 10	5 6 0
1 11	5 9 0
2 0	6 0 0
2 1	6 3 0
2 2	6 6 0
2 3	6 9 0
2 4	7 0 0
2 5	7 3 0
2 6	7 6 0
2 7	7 9 0
2 8	8 0 0
2 9	8 3 0
2 10	8 6 0
2 11	8 9 0
3 0	9 0 0
3 1	9 3 0
3 2	9 6 0
3 3	9 9 0
3 4	10 0 0
3 5	10 3 0
3 6	10 6 0
3 7	10 9 0
3 8	11 0 0
3 9	11 3 0
3 10	11 6 0
3 11	11 9 0
4 0	12 0 0
4 1	12 3 0
4 2	12 6 0
4 3	12 9 0
4 4	13 0 0
4 5	13 3 0
4 6	13 6 0
4 7	13 9 0
4 8	14 0 0
4 9	14 3 0
4 10	14 6 0
4 11	14 9 0
5 0	15 0 0
5 1	15 3 0
5 2	15 6 0
5 3	15 9 0
5 4	16 0 0

3-ft. by

ft. in.	ft. in. pts.
5 5	= 16 3 0
5 6	16 6 0
5 7	16 9 0
5 8	17 0 0
5 9	17 3 0
5 10	17 6 0
5 11	17 9 0
6 0	18 0 0
6 1	18 3 0
6 2	18 6 0
6 3	18 9 0
6 4	19 0 0
6 5	19 3 0
6 6	19 6 0
6 7	19 9 0
6 8	20 0 0
6 9	20 3 0
6 10	20 6 0
6 11	20 9 0
7 0	21 0 0
7 1	21 3 0
7 2	21 6 0
7 3	21 9 0
7 4	22 0 0
7 5	22 3 0
7 6	22 6 0
7 7	22 9 0
7 8	23 0 0
7 9	23 3 0
7 10	23 6 0
7 11	23 9 0
8 0	24 0 0
8 1	24 3 0
8 2	24 6 0
8 3	24 9 0
8 4	25 0 0
8 5	25 3 0
8 6	25 6 0
8 7	25 9 0
8 8	26 0 0
8 9	26 3 0
8 10	26 6 0
8 11	26 9 0
9 0	27 0 0
9 1	27 3 0
9 2	27 6 0
9 3	27 9 0

3-ft. by

ft. in.	ft. in. pts.
9 4	= 28 0 0
9 5	28 3 0
9 6	28 6 0
9 7	28 9 0
9 8	29 0 0
9 9	29 3 0
9 10	29 6 0
9 11	29 9 0
10 0	30 0 0
10 1	30 3 0
10 2	30 6 0
10 3	30 9 0
10 4	31 0 0
10 5	31 3 0
10 6	31 6 0
10 7	31 9 0
10 8	32 0 0
10 9	32 3 0
10 10	32 6 0
10 11	32 9 0
11 0	33 0 0
11 1	33 3 0
11 2	33 6 0
11 3	33 9 0
11 4	34 0 0
11 5	34 3 0
11 6	34 6 0
11 7	34 9 0
11 8	35 0 0
11 9	35 3 0
11 10	35 6 0
11 11	35 9 0
12 0	36 0 0
12 1	36 3 0
12 2	36 6 0
12 3	36 9 0
12 4	37 0 0
12 5	37 3 0
12 6	37 6 0
12 7	37 9 0
12 8	38 0 0
12 9	38 3 0
12 10	38 6 0
12 11	38 9 0
13 0	39 0 0

OF SUPERIOR QUALITY AND MAKE.

C. COLLYER & SON,

3-ft. 1-in.

3-ft. 1-in. by				3-ft. 1-in. by				3-ft. 1-in. by			
ft. in.	ft.	in.	pts.	ft. in.	ft.	in.	pts.	ft. in.	ft.	in.	pts.
1 6	= 4	7	6	5 5	=16	8	5	9 4	=28	9	4
1 7	4	10	7	5 6	16	11	6	9 5	29	0	5
1 8	5	1	8	5 7	17	2	7	9 6	29	3	6
1 9	5	4	9	5 8	17	5	8	9 7	29	6	7
1 10	5	7	10	5 9	17	8	9	9 8	29	9	8
1 11	5	10	11	5 10	17	11	10	9 9	30	0	9
2 0	6	2	0	5 11	18	2	11	9 10	30	3	10
2 1	6	5	1	6 0	18	6	0	9 11	30	6	11
2 2	6	8	2	6 1	18	9	1	10 0	30	10	0
2 3	6	11	3	6 2	19	0	2	10 1	31	1	1
2 4	7	2	4	6 3	19	3	3	10 2	31	4	2
2 5	7	5	5	6 4	19	6	4	10 3	31	7	3
2 6	7	8	6	6 5	19	9	5	10 4	31	10	4
2 7	7	11	7	6 6	20	0	6	10 5	32	1	5
2 8	8	2	8	6 7	20	3	7	10 6	32	4	6
2 9	8	5	9	6 8	20	6	8	10 7	32	7	7
2 10	8	8	10	6 9	20	9	9	10 8	32	10	8
2 11	8	11	11	6 10	21	0	10	10 9	33	1	9
3 0	9	3	0	6 11	21	3	11	10 10	33	4	10
3 1	9	6	1	7 0	21	7	0	10 11	33	7	11
3 2	9	9	2	7 1	21	10	1	11 0	33	11	0
3 3	10	0	3	7 2	22	1	2	11 1	34	2	1
3 4	10	3	4	7 3	22	4	3	11 2	34	5	2
3 5	10	6	5	7 4	22	7	4	11 3	34	8	3
3 6	10	9	6	7 5	22	10	5	11 4	34	11	4
3 7	11	0	7	7 6	23	1	6	11 5	35	2	5
3 8	11	3	8	7 7	23	4	7	11 6	35	5	6
3 9	11	6	9	7 8	23	7	8	11 7	35	8	7
3 10	11	9	10	7 9	23	10	9	11 8	35	11	8
3 11	12	0	11	7 10	24	1	10	11 9	36	2	9
4 0	12	4	0	7 11	24	4	11	11 10	36	5	10
4 1	12	7	1	8 0	24	8	0	11 11	36	8	11
4 2	12	10	2	8 1	24	11	1	12 0	37	0	0
4 3	13	1	3	8 2	25	2	2	12 1	37	3	1
4 4	13	4	4	8 3	25	5	3	12 2	37	6	2
4 5	13	7	5	8 4	25	8	4	12 3	37	9	3
4 6	13	10	6	8 5	25	11	5	12 4	38	0	4
4 7	14	1	7	8 6	26	2	6	12 5	38	3	5
4 8	14	4	8	8 7	26	5	7	12 6	38	6	6
4 9	14	7	9	8 8	26	8	8	12 7	38	9	7
4 10	14	10	10	8 9	26	11	9	12 8	39	0	8
4 11	15	1	11	8 10	27	2	10	12 9	39	3	9
5 0	15	5	0	8 11	27	5	11	12 10	39	6	10
5 1	15	8	1	9 0	27	9	0	12 11	39	9	11
5 2	15	11	2	9 1	28	0	1	13 0	40	1	0
5 3	16	2	3	9 2	28	3	2				
5 4	16	5	4	9 3	28	6	3				

3-ft. 2-in.

3-ft. 2-in. by				3-ft. 2-in. by				3-ft. 2-in. by			
ft. in.	ft.	in.	pts.	ft. in.	ft.	in.	pts.	ft. in.	ft.	in.	pts.
1 6	= 4	9	0	5 5	=17	1	10	9 4	=29	6	8
1 7	5	0	2	5 6	17	5	0	9 5	29	9	10
1 8	5	3	4	5 7	17	8	2	9 6	30	1	0
1 9	5	6	6	5 8	17	11	4	9 7	30	4	2
1 10	5	9	8	5 9	18	2	6	9 8	30	7	4
1 11	6	0	10	5 10	18	5	8	9 9	30	10	6
2 0	6	4	0	5 11	18	8	10	9 10	31	1	8
2 1	6	7	2	6 0	19	0	0	9 11	31	4	10
2 2	6	10	4	6 1	19	3	2	10 0	31	8	0
2 3	7	1	6	6 2	19	6	4	10 1	31	11	2
2 4	7	4	8	6 3	19	9	6	10 2	32	2	4
2 5	7	7	10	6 4	20	0	8	10 3	32	5	6
2 6	7	11	0	6 5	20	3	10	10 4	32	8	8
2 7	8	2	2	6 6	20	7	0	10 5	32	11	10
2 8	8	5	4	6 7	20	10	2	10 6	33	3	0
2 9	8	8	6	6 8	21	1	4	10 7	33	6	2
2 10	8	11	8	6 9	21	4	6	10 8	33	9	4
2 11	9	2	10	6 10	21	7	8	10 9	34	0	6
3 0	9	6	0	6 11	21	10	10	10 10	34	3	8
3 1	9	9	2	7 0	22	2	0	10 11	34	6	10
3 2	10	0	4	7 1	22	5	2	11 0	34	10	0
3 3	10	3	6	7 2	22	8	4	11 1	35	1	2
3 4	10	6	8	7 3	22	11	6	11 2	35	4	4
3 5	10	9	10	7 4	23	2	8	11 3	35	7	6
3 6	11	1	0	7 5	23	5	10	11 4	35	10	8
3 7	11	4	2	7 6	23	9	0	11 5	36	1	10
3 8	11	7	4	7 7	24	0	2	11 6	36	5	0
3 9	11	10	6	7 8	24	3	4	11 7	36	8	2
3 10	12	1	8	7 9	24	6	6	11 8	36	11	4
3 11	12	4	10	7 10	24	9	8	11 9	37	2	6
4 0	12	8	0	7 11	25	0	10	11 10	37	5	8
4 1	12	11	2	8 0	25	4	0	11 11	37	8	10
4 2	13	2	4	8 1	25	7	2	12 0	38	0	0
4 3	13	5	6	8 2	25	10	4	12 1	38	3	2
4 4	13	8	8	8 3	26	1	6	12 2	38	6	4
4 5	13	11	10	8 4	26	4	8	12 3	38	9	6
4 6	14	3	0	8 5	26	7	10	12 4	39	0	8
4 7	14	6	2	8 6	26	11	0	12 5	39	3	10
4 8	14	9	4	8 7	27	2	2	12 6	39	7	0
4 9	15	0	6	8 8	27	5	4	12 7	39	10	2
4 10	15	3	8	8 9	27	8	6	12 8	40	1	4
4 11	15	6	10	8 10	27	11	8	12 9	40	4	6
5 0	15	10	0	8 11	28	2	10	12 10	40	7	8
5 1	16	1	2	9 0	28	6	0	12 11	40	10	10
5 2	16	4	4	9 1	28	9	2	13 0	41	2	0
5 3	16	7	6	9 2	29	0	4				
5 4	16	10	8	9 3	29	3	6				

ON AN IMPROVED PRINCIPLE.

3-ft. 3-in.

3-ft. 3-in. by				3-ft. 3-in. by				3-ft. 3-in. by			
ft. in.	ft.	in.	pts.	ft. in.	ft.	in.	pts.	ft. in.	ft.	in.	pts.
1 6	= 4	10	6	5 5	=17	7	3	9 4	=30	4	0
1 7	5	1	9	5 6	17	10	6	9 5	30	7	3
1 8	5	5	0	5 7	18	1	9	9 6	30	10	6
1 9	5	8	3	5 8	18	5	0	9 7	31	1	9
1 10	5	11	6	5 9	18	8	3	9 8	31	5	0
1 11	6	2	9	5 10	18	11	6	9 9	31	8	3
2 0	6	6	0	5 11	19	2	9	9 10	31	11	6
2 1	6	9	3	6 0	19	6	0	9 11	32	2	9
2 2	7	0	6	6 1	19	9	3	10 0	32	6	0
2 3	7	3	9	6 2	20	0	6	10 1	32	9	3
2 4	7	7	0	6 3	20	3	9	10 2	33	0	6
2 5	7	10	3	6 4	20	7	0	10 3	33	3	9
2 6	8	1	6	6 5	20	10	3	10 4	33	7	0
2 7	8	4	9	6 6	21	1	6	10 5	33	10	3
2 8	8	8	0	6 7	21	4	9	10 6	34	1	6
2 9	8	11	3	6 8	21	8	0	10 7	34	4	9
2 10	9	2	6	6 9	21	11	3	10 8	34	8	0
2 11	9	5	9	6 10	22	2	6	10 9	34	11	3
3 0	9	9	0	6 11	22	5	9	10 10	35	2	6
3 1	10	0	3	7 0	22	9	0	10 11	35	5	9
3 2	10	3	6	7 1	23	0	3	11 0	35	9	0
3 3	10	6	9	7 2	23	3	6	11 1	36	0	3
3 4	10	10	0	7 3	23	6	9	11 2	36	3	6
3 5	11	1	3	7 4	23	10	0	11 3	36	6	9
3 6	11	4	6	7 5	24	1	3	11 4	36	10	0
3 7	11	7	9	7 6	24	4	6	11 5	37	1	3
3 8	11	11	0	7 7	24	7	9	11 6	37	4	6
3 9	12	2	3	7 8	24	11	0	11 7	37	7	9
3 10	12	5	6	7 9	25	2	3	11 8	37	11	0
3 11	12	8	9	7 10	25	5	6	11 9	38	2	3
4 0	13	0	0	7 11	25	8	9	11 10	38	5	6
4 1	13	3	3	8 0	26	0	0	11 11	38	8	9
4 2	13	6	6	8 1	26	3	3	12 0	39	0	0
4 3	13	9	9	8 2	26	6	6	12 1	39	3	3
4 4	14	1	0	8 3	26	9	9	12 2	39	6	6
4 5	14	4	3	8 4	27	1	0	12 3	39	9	9
4 6	14	7	6	8 5	27	4	3	12 4	40	1	0
4 7	14	10	9	8 6	27	7	6	12 5	40	4	3
4 8	15	2	0	8 7	27	10	9	12 6	40	7	6
4 9	15	5	3	8 8	28	2	0	12 7	40	10	9
4 10	15	8	6	8 9	28	5	3	12 8	41	2	0
4 11	15	11	9	8 10	28	8	6	12 9	41	5	3
5 0	16	3	0	8 11	28	11	9	12 10	41	8	6
5 1	16	6	3	9 0	29	3	0	12 11	41	11	9
5 2	16	9	6	9 1	29	6	3	13 0	42	3	0
5 3	17	0	9	9 2	29	9	6				
5 4	17	4	0	9 3	30	0	9				

3-ft. 4-in.

3-ft. 4-in. by

ft. in.	ft. in. pts.
1 6	= 5 0 0
1 7	5 3 4
1 8	5 6 8
1 9	5 10 0
1 10	6 1 4
1 11	6 4 8
2 0	6 8 0
2 1	6 11 4
2 2	7 2 8
2 3	7 6 0
2 4	7 9 4
2 5	8 0 8
2 6	8 4 0
2 7	8 7 4
2 8	8 10 8
2 9	9 2 0
2 10	9 5 4
2 11	9 8 8
3 0	10 0 0
3 1	10 3 4
3 2	10 6 8
3 3	10 10 0
3 4	11 1 4
3 5	11 4 8
3 6	11 8 0
3 7	11 11 4
3 8	12 2 8
3 9	12 6 0
3 10	12 9 4
3 11	13 0 8
4 0	13 4 0
4 1	13 7 4
4 2	13 10 8
4 3	14 2 0
4 4	14 5 4
4 5	14 8 8
4 6	15 0 0
4 7	15 3 4
4 8	15 6 8
4 9	15 10 0
4 10	16 1 4
4 11	16 4 8
5 0	16 8 0
5 1	16 11 4
5 2	17 2 8
5 3	17 6 0
5 4	17 9 4

3-ft. 4-in. by

ft. in.	ft. in. pts.
5 5	= 18 0 8
5 6	18 4 0
5 7	18 7 4
5 8	18 10 8
5 9	19 2 0
5 10	19 5 4
5 11	19 8 8
6 0	20 0 0
6 1	20 3 4
6 2	20 6 8
6 3	20 10 0
6 4	21 1 4
6 5	21 4 8
6 6	21 8 0
6 7	21 11 4
6 8	22 2 8
6 9	22 6 0
6 10	22 9 4
6 11	23 0 8
7 0	23 4 0
7 1	23 7 4
7 2	23 10 8
7 3	24 2 0
7 4	24 5 4
7 5	24 8 8
7 6	25 0 0
7 7	25 3 4
7 8	25 6 8
7 9	25 10 0
7 10	26 1 4
7 11	26 4 8
8 0	26 8 0
8 1	26 11 4
8 2	27 2 8
8 3	27 6 0
8 4	27 9 4
8 5	28 0 8
8 6	28 4 0
8 7	28 7 4
8 8	28 10 8
8 9	29 2 0
8 10	29 5 4
8 11	29 8 8
9 0	30 0 0
9 1	30 3 4
9 2	30 6 8
9 3	30 10 0

3-ft. 4-in. by

ft. in.	ft. in. pts.
9 4	= 31 1 4
9 5	31 4 8
9 6	31 8 0
9 7	31 11 4
9 8	32 2 8
9 9	32 6 0
9 10	32 9 4
9 11	33 0 8
10 0	33 4 0
10 1	33 7 4
10 2	33 10 8
10 3	34 2 0
10 4	34 5 4
10 5	34 8 8
10 6	35 0 0
10 7	35 3 4
10 8	35 6 8
10 9	35 10 0
10 10	36 1 4
10 11	36 4 8
11 0	36 8 0
11 1	36 11 4
11 2	37 2 8
11 3	37 6 0
11 4	37 9 4
11 5	38 0 8
11 6	38 4 0
11 7	38 7 4
11 8	38 10 8
11 9	39 2 0
11 10	39 5 4
11 11	39 8 8
12 0	40 0 0
12 1	40 3 4
12 2	40 6 8
12 3	40 10 0
12 4	41 1 4
12 5	41 4 8
12 6	41 8 0
12 7	41 11 4
12 8	42 2 8
12 9	42 6 0
12 10	42 9 4
12 11	43 0 8
13 0	43 4 0

FOR GARDEN ENTRANCES.

3-ft. 5-in.

3-ft. 5-in. by

ft. in.	ft. in. pts.
1 6	= 5 1 6
1 7	5 4 11
1 8	5 8 4
1 9	5 11 9
1 10	6 3 2
1 11	6 6 7
2 0	6 10 0
2 1	7 1 5
2 2	7 4 10
2 3	7 8 3
2 4	7 11 8
2 5	8 3 1
2 6	8 6 6
2 7	8 9 11
2 8	9 1 4
2 9	9 4 9
2 10	9 8 2
2 11	9 11 7
3 0	10 3 0
3 1	10 6 5
3 2	10 9 10
3 3	11 1 3
3 4	11 4 8
3 5	11 8 1
3 6	11 11 6
3 7	12 2 11
3 8	12 6 4
3 9	12 9 9
3 10	13 1 2
3 11	13 4 7
4 0	13 8 0
4 1	13 11 5
4 2	14 2 10
4 3	14 6 3
4 4	14 9 8
4 5	15 1 1
4 6	15 4 6
4 7	15 7 11
4 8	15 11 4
4 9	16 2 9
4 10	16 6 2
4 11	16 9 7
5 0	17 1 0
5 1	17 4 5
5 2	17 7 10
5 3	17 11 3
5 4	18 2 8

3-ft. 5-in. by

ft. in.	ft. in. pts.
5 5	=18 6 1
5 6	18 9 6
5 7	19 0 11
5 8	19 4 4
5 9	19 7 9
5 10	19 11 2
5 11	20 2 7
6 0	20 6 0
6 1	20 9 5
6 2	21 0 10
6 3	21 4 3
6 4	21 7 8
6 5	21 11 1
6 6	22 2 6
6 7	22 5 11
6 8	22 9 4
6 9	23 0 9
6 10	23 4 2
6 11	23 7 7
7 0	23 11 0
7 1	24 2 5
7 2	24 5 10
7 3	24 9 3
7 4	25 0 8
7 5	25 4 1
7 6	25 7 6
7 7	25 10 11
7 8	26 2 4
7 9	26 5 9
7 10	26 9 2
7 11	27 0 7
8 0	27 4 0
8 1	27 7 5
8 2	27 10 10
8 3	28 2 3
8 4	28 5 8
8 5	28 9 1
8 6	29 0 6
8 7	29 3 11
8 8	29 7 4
8 9	29 10 9
8 10	30 2 2
8 11	30 5 7
9 0	30 9 0
9 1	31 0 5
9 2	31 3 10
9 3	31 7 3

3-ft. 5-in. by

ft. in.	ft. in. pts.
9 4	=31 10 8
9 5	32 2 1
9 6	32 5 6
9 7	32 8 11
9 8	33 0 4
9 9	33 3 9
9 10	33 7 2
9 11	33 10 7
10 0	34 2 0
10 1	34 5 5
10 2	34 8 10
10 3	35 0 3
10 4	35 3 8
10 5	35 7 1
10 6	35 10 6
10 7	36 1 11
10 8	36 5 4
10 9	36 8 9
10 10	37 0 2
10 11	37 3 7
11 0	37 7 0
11 1	37 10 5
11 2	38 1 10
11 3	38 5 3
11 4	38 8 8
11 5	39 0 1
11 6	39 3 6
11 7	39 6 11
11 8	39 10 4
11 9	40 1 9
11 10	40 5 2
11 11	40 8 7
12 0	41 0 0
12 1	41 3 5
12 2	41 6 10
12 3	41 10 3
12 4	42 1 8
12 5	42 5 1
12 6	42 8 6
12 7	42 11 11
12 8	43 3 4
12 9	43 6 9
12 10	43 10 2
12 11	44 1 7
13 0	44 5 0

3-ft. 6-in.

3-ft. 6-in. by			3-ft. 6-in. by			3-ft. 6-in. by		
ft. in.	ft. in.	pts.	ft. in.	ft. in.	pts.	ft. in.	ft. in.	pts.
1 6	= 5 3	0	5 5	=18 11	6	9 4	=32 8	0
1 7	5 6	6	5 6	19 3	0	9 5	32 11	6
1 8	5 10	0	5 7	19 6	6	9 6	33 3	0
1 9	6 1	6	5 8	19 10	0	9 7	33 6	6
1 10	6 5	0	5 9	20 1	6	9 8	33 10	0
1 11	6 8	6	5 10	20 5	0	9 9	34 1	6
2 0	7 0	0	5 11	20 8	6	9 10	34 5	0
2 1	7 3	6	6 0	21 0	0	9 11	34 8	6
2 2	7 7	0	6 1	21 3	6	10 0	35 0	0
2 3	7 10	6	6 2	21 7	0	10 1	35 3	6
2 4	8 2	0	6 3	21 10	6	10 2	35 7	0
2 5	8 5	6	6 4	22 2	0	10 3	35 10	6
2 6	8 9	0	6 5	22 5	6	10 4	36 2	0
2 7	9 0	6	6 6	22 9	0	10 5	36 5	6
2 8	9 4	0	6 7	23 0	6	10 6	36 9	0
2 9	9 7	6	6 8	23 4	0	10 7	37 0	6
2 10	9 11	0	6 9	23 7	6	10 8	37 4	0
2 11	10 2	6	6 10	23 11	0	10 9	37 7	6
3 0	10 6	0	6 11	24 2	6	10 10	37 11	0
3 1	10 9	6	7 0	24 6	0	10 11	38 2	6
3 2	11 1	0	7 1	24 9	6	11 0	38 6	0
3 3	11 4	6	7 2	25 1	0	11 1	38 9	6
3 4	11 8	0	7 3	25 4	6	11 2	39 1	0
3 5	11 11	6	7 4	25 8	0	11 3	39 4	6
3 6	12 3	0	7 5	25 11	6	11 4	39 8	0
3 7	12 6	6	7 6	26 3	0	11 5	39 11	6
3 8	12 10	0	7 7	26 6	6	11 6	40 3	0
3 9	13 1	6	7 8	26 10	0	11 7	40 6	6
3 10	13 5	0	7 9	27 1	6	11 8	40 10	0
3 11	13 8	6	7 10	27 5	0	11 9	41 1	6
4 0	14 0	0	7 11	27 8	6	11 10	41 5	0
4 1	14 3	6	8 0	28 0	0	11 11	41 8	6
4 2	14 7	0	8 1	28 3	6	12 0	42 0	0
4 3	14 10	6	8 2	28 7	0	12 1	42 3	6
4 4	15 2	0	8 3	28 10	6	12 2	42 7	0
4 5	15 5	6	8 4	29 2	0	12 3	42 10	6
4 6	15 9	0	8 5	29 5	6	12 4	43 2	0
4 7	16 0	6	8 6	29 9	0	12 5	43 5	6
4 8	16 4	0	8 7	30 0	6	12 6	43 9	0
4 9	16 7	6	8 8	30 4	0	12 7	44 0	6
4 10	16 11	0	8 9	30 7	6	12 8	44 4	0
4 11	17 2	6	8 10	30 11	0	12 9	44 7	6
5 0	17 6	0	8 11	31 2	6	12 10	44 11	0
5 1	17 9	6	9 0	31 6	0	12 11	45 2	6
5 2	18 1	0	9 1	31 9	6	13 0	45 6	0
5 3	18 4	6	9 2	32 1	0			
5 4	18 8	0	9 3	32 4	6			

AND PATTERNS SENT.

3-ft. 7-in.

3-ft. 7-in. by				3-ft. 7-in. by				3-ft. 7-in. by		
ft. in.	ft.	in.	pts.	ft. in.	ft.	in.	pts.	ft. in.	ft.	in.	pts.
1 6	= 5	4	6	5 5	= 19	4	11	9 4	= 33	5	4
1 7	5	8	1	5 6	19	8	6	9 5	33	8	11
1 8	5	11	8	5 7	20	0	1	9 6	34	0	6
1 9	6	3	3	5 8	20	3	8	9 7	34	4	1
1 10	6	6	10	5 9	20	7	3	9 8	34	7	8
1 11	6	10	5	5 10	20	10	10	9 9	34	11	3
2 0	7	2	0	5 11	21	2	5	9 10	35	2	10
2 1	7	5	7	6 0	21	6	0	9 11	35	6	5
2 2	7	9	2	6 1	21	9	7	10 0	35	10	0
2 3	8	0	9	6 2	22	1	2	10 1	36	1	7
2 4	8	4	4	6 3	22	4	9	10 2	36	5	2
2 5	8	7	11	6 4	22	8	4	10 3	36	8	9
2 6	8	11	6	6 5	22	11	11	10 4	37	0	4
2 7	9	3	1	6 6	23	3	6	10 5	37	3	11
2 8	9	6	8	6 7	23	7	1	10 6	37	7	6
2 9	9	10	3	6 8	23	10	8	10 7	37	11	1
2 10	10	1	10	6 9	24	2	3	10 8	38	2	8
2 11	10	5	5	6 10	24	5	10	10 9	38	6	3
3 0	10	9	0	6 11	24	9	5	10 10	38	9	10
3 1	11	0	7	7 0	25	1	0	10 11	39	1	5
3 2	11	4	2	7 1	25	4	7	11 0	39	5	0
3 3	11	7	9	7 2	25	8	2	11 1	39	8	7
3 4	11	11	4	7 3	25	11	9	11 2	40	0	2
3 5	12	2	11	7 4	26	3	4	11 3	40	3	9
3 6	12	6	6	7 5	26	6	11	11 4	40	7	4
3 7	12	10	1	7 6	26	10	6	11 5	40	10	11
3 8	13	1	8	7 7	27	2	1	11 6	41	2	6
3 9	13	5	3	7 8	27	5	8	11 7	41	6	1
3 10	13	8	10	7 9	27	9	3	11 8	41	9	8
3 11	14	0	5	7 10	28	0	10	11 9	42	1	3
4 0	14	4	0	7 11	28	4	5	11 10	42	4	10
4 1	14	7	7	8 0	28	8	0	11 11	42	8	5
4 2	14	11	2	8 1	28	11	7	12 0	43	0	0
4 3	15	2	9	8 2	29	3	2	12 1	43	3	7
4 4	15	6	4	8 3	29	6	9	12 2	43	7	2
4 5	15	9	11	8 4	29	10	4	12 3	43	10	9
4 6	16	1	6	8 5	30	1	11	12 4	44	2	4
4 7	16	5	1	8 6	30	5	6	12 5	44	5	11
4 8	16	8	8	8 7	30	9	1	12 6	44	9	6
4 9	17	0	3	8 8	31	0	8	12 7	45	1	1
4 10	17	3	10	8 9	31	4	3	12 8	45	4	8
4 11	17	7	5	8 10	31	7	10	12 9	45	8	3
5 0	17	11	0	8 11	31	11	5	12 10	45	11	10
5 1	18	2	7	9 0	32	3	0	12 11	46	3	5
5 2	18	6	2	9 1	32	6	7	13 0	46	7	0
5 3	18	9	9	9 2	32	10	2				
5 4	19	1	4	9 3	33	1	9				

36, FARRINGDON STREET, LONDON, E.C.

AWNINGS FITTED

3-ft. 8-in.

3-ft. 8-in. by				3-ft. 8-in. by				3-ft. 8-in. by			
ft. in.	ft.	in.	pts.	ft. in.	ft.	in.	pts.	ft. in.	ft.	in.	pts.
1 6	= 5	6	0	5 5	=19	10	4	9 4	=34	2	8
1 7	5	9	8	5 6	20	2	0	9 5	34	6	4
1 8	6	1	4	5 7	20	5	8	9 6	34	10	0
1 9	6	5	0	5 8	20	9	4	9 7	35	1	8
1 10	6	8	8	5 9	21	1	0	9 8	35	5	4
1 11	7	0	4	5 10	21	4	8	9 9	35	9	0
2 0	7	4	0	5 11	21	8	4	9 10	36	0	8
2 1	7	7	8	6 0	22	0	0	9 11	36	4	4
2 2	7	11	4	6 1	22	3	8	10 0	36	8	0
2 3	8	3	0	6 2	22	7	4	10 1	36	11	8
2 4	8	6	8	6 3	22	11	0	10 2	37	3	4
2 5	8	10	4	6 4	23	2	8	10 3	37	7	0
2 6	9	2	0	6 5	23	6	4	10 4	37	10	8
2 7	9	5	8	6 6	23	10	0	10 5	38	2	4
2 8	9	9	4	6 7	24	1	8	10 6	38	6	0
2 9	10	1	0	6 8	24	5	4	10 7	38	9	8
2 10	10	4	8	6 9	24	9	0	10 8	39	1	4
2 11	10	8	4	6 10	25	0	8	10 9	39	5	0
3 0	11	0	0	6 11	25	4	4	10 10	39	8	8
3 1	11	3	8	7 0	25	8	0	10 11	40	0	4
3 2	11	7	4	7 1	25	11	8	11 0	40	4	0
3 3	11	11	0	7 2	26	3	4	11 1	40	7	8
3 4	12	2	8	7 3	26	7	0	11 2	40	11	4
3 5	12	6	4	7 4	26	10	8	11 3	41	3	0
3 6	12	10	0	7 5	27	2	4	11 4	41	6	8
3 7	13	1	8	7 6	27	6	0	11 5	41	10	4
3 8	13	5	4	7 7	27	9	8	11 6	42	2	0
3 9	13	9	0	7 8	28	1	4	11 7	42	5	8
3 10	14	0	8	7 9	28	5	0	11 8	42	9	4
3 11	14	4	4	7 10	28	8	8	11 9	43	1	0
4 0	14	8	0	7 11	29	0	4	11 10	43	4	8
4 1	14	11	8	8 0	29	4	0	11 11	43	8	4
4 2	15	3	4	8 1	29	7	8	12 0	44	0	0
4 3	15	7	0	8 2	29	11	4	12 1	44	3	8
4 4	15	10	8	8 3	30	3	0	12 2	44	7	4
4 5	16	2	4	8 4	30	6	8	12 3	44	11	0
4 6	16	6	0	8 5	30	10	4	12 4	45	2	8
4 7	16	9	8	8 6	31	2	0	12 5	45	6	4
4 8	17	1	4	8 7	31	5	8	12 6	45	10	0
4 9	17	5	0	8 8	31	9	4	12 7	46	1	8
4 10	17	8	8	8 9	32	1	0	12 8	46	5	4
4 11	18	0	4	8 10	32	4	8	12 9	46	9	0
5 0	18	4	0	8 11	32	8	4	12 10	47	0	8
5 1	18	7	8	9 0	33	0	0	12 11	47	4	4
5 2	18	11	4	9 1	33	3	8	13 0	47	8	0
5 3	19	3	0	9 2	33	7	4				
5 4	19	6	8	9 3	33	11	0				

TO VERANDAHS AND PORTICOS:

3-ft. 9-in.

3-ft. 9-in. by

ft. in.	ft. in. pts.	ft. in.	ft. in. pts.	ft. in.	ft. in. pts.
1 6	= 5 7 6	5 5	=20 3 9	9 4	=35 0 0
1 7	5 11 3	5 6	20 7 6	9 5	35 3 9
1 8	6 3 0	5 7	20 11 3	9 6	35 7 6
1 9	6 6 9	5 8	21 3 0	9 7	35 11 3
1 10	6 10 6	5 9	21 6 9	9 8	36 3 0
1 11	7 2 3	5 10	21 10 6	9 9	36 6 9
2 0	7 6 0	5 11	22 2 3	9 10	36 10 6
2 1	7 9 9	6 0	22 6 0	9 11	37 2 3
2 2	8 1 6	6 1	22 9 9	10 0	37 6 0
2 3	8 5 3	6 2	23 1 6	10 1	37 9 9
2 4	8 9 0	6 3	23 5 3	10 2	38 1 6
2 5	9 0 9	6 4	23 9 0	10 3	38 5 3
2 6	9 4 6	6 5	24 0 9	10 4	38 9 0
2 7	9 8 3	6 6	24 4 6	10 5	39 0 9
2 8	10 0 0	6 7	24 8 3	10 6	39 4 6
2 9	10 3 9	6 8	25 0 0	10 7	39 8 3
2 10	10 7 6	6 9	25 3 9	10 8	40 0 0
2 11	10 11 3	6 10	25 7 6	10 9	40 3 9
3 0	11 3 0	6 11	25 11 3	10 10	40 7 6
3 1	11 6 9	7 0	26 3 0	10 11	40 11 3
3 2	11 10 6	7 1	26 6 9	11 0	41 3 0
3 3	12 2 3	7 2	26 10 6	11 1	41 6 9
3 4	12 6 0	7 3	27 2 3	11 2	41 10 6
3 5	12 9 9	7 4	27 6 0	11 3	42 2 3
3 6	13 1 6	7 5	27 9 9	11 4	42 6 0
3 7	13 5 3	7 6	28 1 6	11 5	42 9 9
3 8	13 9 0	7 7	28 5 3	11 6	43 1 6
3 9	14 0 9	7 8	28 9 0	11 7	43 5 3
3 10	14 4 6	7 9	29 0 9	11 8	43 9 0
3 11	14 8 3	7 10	29 4 6	11 9	44 0 9
4 0	15 0 0	7 11	29 8 3	11 10	44 4 6
4 1	15 3 9	8 0	30 0 0	11 11	44 8 3
4 2	15 7 6	8 1	30 3 9	12 0	45 0 0
4 3	15 11 3	8 2	30 7 6	12 1	45 3 9
4 4	16 3 0	8 3	30 11 3	12 2	45 7 6
4 5	16 6 9	8 4	31 3 0	12 3	45 11 3
4 6	16 10 6	8 5	31 6 9	12 4	46 3 0
4 7	17 2 3	8 6	31 10 6	12 5	46 6 9
4 8	17 6 0	8 7	32 2 3	12 6	46 10 6
4 9	17 9 9	8 8	32 6 0	12 7	47 2 3
4 10	18 1 6	8 9	32 9 9	12 8	47 6 0
4 11	18 5 3	8 10	33 1 6	12 9	47 9 9
5 0	18 9 0	8 11	33 5 3	12 10	48 1 6
5 1	19 0 9	9 0	33 9 0	12 11	48 5 3
5 2	19 4 6	9 1	34 0 9	13 0	48 9 0
5 3	19 8 3	9 2	34 4 6		
5 4	20 0 0	9 3	34 8 3		

3-ft. 10-in.

3-ft. 10-in. by				3-ft. 10-in. by				3-ft. 10-in. by		
ft. in.	ft.	in.	pts.	ft. in.	ft.	in.	pts.	ft. in.	ft.	in.	pts.
1 6 =	5	9	0	5 5 =	20	9	2	9 4 =	35	9	4
1 7	6	0	10	5 6	21	1	0	9 5	36	1	2
1 8	6	4	8	5 7	21	4	10	9 6	36	5	0
1 9	6	8	6	5 8	21	8	8	9 7	36	8	10
1 10	7	0	4	5 9	22	0	6	9 8	37	0	8
1 11	7	4	2	5 10	22	4	4	9 9	37	4	6
2 0	7	8	0	5 11	22	8	2	9 10	37	8	4
2 1	7	11	10	6 0	23	0	0	9 11	38	0	2
2 2	8	3	8	6 1	23	3	10	10 0	38	4	0
2 3	8	7	6	6 2	23	7	8	10 1	38	7	10
2 4	8	11	4	6 3	23	11	6	10 2	38	11	8
2 5	9	3	2	6 4	24	3	4	10 3	39	3	6
2 6	9	7	0	6 5	24	7	2	10 4	39	7	4
2 7	9	10	10	6 6	24	11	0	10 5	39	11	2
2 8	10	2	8	6 7	25	2	10	10 6	40	3	0
2 9	10	6	6	6 8	25	6	8	10 7	40	6	10
2 10	10	10	4	6 9	25	10	6	10 8	40	10	8
2 11	11	2	2	6 10	26	2	4	10 9	41	2	6
3 0	11	6	0	6 11	26	6	2	10 10	41	6	4
3 1	11	9	10	7 0	26	10	0	10 11	41	10	2
3 2	12	1	8	7 1	27	1	10	11 0	42	2	0
3 3	12	5	6	7 2	27	5	8	11 1	42	5	10
3 4	12	9	4	7 3	27	9	6	11 2	42	9	8
3 5	13	1	2	7 4	28	1	4	11 3	43	1	6
3 6	13	5	0	7 5	28	5	2	11 4	43	5	4
3 7	13	8	10	7 6	28	9	0	11 5	43	9	2
3 8	14	0	8	7 7	29	0	10	11 6	44	1	0
3 9	14	4	6	7 8	29	4	8	11 7	44	4	10
3 10	14	8	4	7 9	29	8	6	11 8	44	8	8
3 11	15	0	2	7 10	30	0	4	11 9	45	0	6
4 0	15	4	0	7 11	30	4	2	11 10	45	4	4
4 1	15	7	10	8 0	30	8	0	11 11	45	8	2
4 2	15	11	8	8 1	30	11	10	12 0	46	0	0
4 3	16	3	6	8 2	31	3	8	12 1	46	3	10
4 4	16	7	4	8 3	31	7	6	12 2	46	7	8
4 5	16	11	2	8 4	31	11	4	12 3	46	11	6
4 6	17	3	0	8 5	32	3	2	12 4	47	3	4
4 7	17	6	10	8 6	32	7	0	12 5	47	7	2
4 8	17	10	8	8 7	32	10	10	12 6	47	11	0
4 9	18	2	6	8 8	33	2	8	12 7	48	2	10
4 10	18	6	4	8 9	33	6	6	12 8	48	6	8
4 11	18	10	2	8 10	33	10	4	12 9	48	10	6
5 0	19	2	0	8 11	34	2	2	12 10	49	2	4
5 1	19	5	10	9 0	34	6	0	12 11	49	6	2
5 2	19	9	8	9 1	34	9	10	13 0	49	10	0
5 3	20	1	6	9 2	35	1	8				
5 4	20	5	4	9 3	35	5	6				

3-ft. 11-in.

3-ft. 11-in. by				3-ft. 11-in. by				3-ft. 11-in. by			
ft.	in.	ft.	in. pts.	ft.	in.	ft.	in pts.	ft.	in.	ft.	in. pts.
1	6	= 5	10 6	5	5	=21	2 7	9	4	=36	6 8
1	7	6	2 5	5	6	21	6 6	9	5	36	10 7
1	8	6	6 4	5	7	21	10 5	9	6	37	2 6
1	9	6	10 3	5	8	22	2 4	9	7	37	6 5
1	10	7	2 2	5	9	22	6 3	9	8	37	10 4
1	11	7	6 1	5	10	22	10 2	9	9	38	2 3
2	0	7	10 0	5	11	23	2 1	9	10	38	6 2
2	1	8	1 11	6	0	23	6 0	9	11	38	10 1
2	2	8	5 10	6	1	23	9 11	10	0	39	2 0
2	3	8	9 9	6	2	24	1 10	10	1	39	5 11
2	4	9	1 8	6	3	24	5 9	10	2	39	9 10
2	5	9	5 7	6	4	24	9 8	10	3	40	1 9
2	6	9	9 6	6	5	25	1 7	10	4	40	5 8
2	7	10	1 5	6	6	25	5 6	10	5	40	9 7
2	8	10	5 4	6	7	25	9 5	10	6	41	1 6
2	9	10	9 3	6	8	26	1 4	10	7	41	5 5
2	10	11	1 2	6	9	26	5 3	10	8	41	9 4
2	11	11	5 1	6	10	26	9 2	10	9	42	1 3
3	0	11	9 0	6	11	27	1 1	10	10	42	5 2
3	1	12	0 11	7	0	27	5 0	10	11	42	9 1
3	2	12	4 10	7	1	27	8 11	11	0	43	1 0
3	3	12	8 9	7	2	28	0 10	11	1	43	4 11
3	4	13	0 8	7	3	28	4 9	11	2	43	8 10
3	5	13	4 7	7	4	28	8 8	11	3	44	0 9
3	6	13	8 6	7	5	29	0 7	11	4	44	4 8
3	7	14	0 5	7	6	29	4 6	11	5	44	8 7
3	8	14	4 4	7	7	29	8 5	11	6	45	0 6
3	9	14	8 3	7	8	30	0 4	11	7	45	4 5
3	10	15	0 2	7	9	30	4 3	11	8	45	8 4
3	11	15	4 1	7	10	30	8 2	11	9	46	0 3
4	0	15	8 0	7	11	31	0 1	11	10	46	4 2
4	1	15	11 11	8	0	31	4 0	11	11	46	8 1
4	2	16	3 10	8	1	31	7 11	12	0	47	0 0
4	3	16	7 9	8	2	31	11 10	12	1	47	3 11
4	4	16	11 8	8	3	32	3 9	12	2	47	7 10
4	5	17	3 7	8	4	32	7 8	12	3	47	11 9
4	6	17	7 6	8	5	32	11 7	12	4	48	3 8
4	7	17	11 5	8	6	33	3 6	12	5	48	7 7
4	8	18	3 4	8	7	33	7 5	12	6	48	11 6
4	9	18	7 3	8	8	33	11 4	12	7	49	3 5
4	10	18	11 2	8	9	34	3 3	12	8	49	7 4
4	11	19	3 1	8	10	34	7 2	12	9	49	11 3
5	0	19	7 0	8	11	34	11 1	12	10	50	3 2
5	1	19	10 11	9	0	35	3 0	12	11	50	7 1
5	2	20	2 10	9	1	35	6 11	13	0	50	11 0
5	3	20	6 9	9	2	35	10 10				
5	4	20	10 8	9	3	36	2 9				

4-ft.

4-ft. by					4-ft. by					4-ft. by				
ft.	in.	ft.	in.	pts.	ft.	in.	ft.	in.	pts.	ft.	in.	ft.	in.	pts.
1	6	= 6	0	0	5	5	=21	8	0	9	4	=37	4	0
1	7	6	4	0	5	6	22	0	0	9	5	37	8	0
1	8	6	8	0	5	7	22	4	0	9	6	38	0	0
1	9	7	0	0	5	8	22	8	0	9	7	38	4	0
1	10	7	4	0	5	9	23	0	0	9	8	38	8	0
1	11	7	8	0	5	10	23	4	0	9	9	39	0	0
2	0	8	0	0	5	11	23	8	0	9	10	39	4	0
2	1	8	4	0	6	0	24	0	0	9	11	39	8	0
2	2	8	8	0	6	1	24	4	0	10	0	40	0	0
2	3	9	0	0	6	2	24	8	0	10	1	40	4	0
2	4	9	4	0	6	3	25	0	0	10	2	40	8	0
2	5	9	8	0	6	4	25	4	0	10	3	41	0	0
2	6	10	0	0	6	5	25	8	0	10	4	41	4	0
2	7	10	4	0	6	6	26	0	0	10	5	41	8	0
2	8	10	8	0	6	7	26	4	0	10	6	42	0	0
2	9	11	0	0	6	8	26	8	0	10	7	42	4	0
2	10	11	4	0	6	9	27	0	0	10	8	42	8	0
2	11	11	8	0	6	10	27	4	0	10	9	43	0	0
3	0	12	0	0	6	11	27	8	0	10	10	43	4	0
3	1	12	4	0	7	0	28	0	0	10	11	43	8	0
3	2	12	8	0	7	1	28	4	0	11	0	44	0	0
3	3	13	0	0	7	2	28	8	0	11	1	44	4	0
3	4	13	4	0	7	3	29	0	0	11	2	44	8	0
3	5	13	8	0	7	4	29	4	0	11	3	45	0	0
3	6	14	0	0	7	5	29	8	0	11	4	45	4	0
3	7	14	4	0	7	6	30	0	0	11	5	45	8	0
3	8	14	8	0	7	7	30	4	0	11	6	46	0	0
3	9	15	0	0	7	8	30	8	0	11	7	46	4	0
3	10	15	4	0	7	9	31	0	0	11	8	46	8	0
3	11	15	8	0	7	10	31	4	0	11	9	47	0	0
4	0	16	0	0	7	11	31	8	0	11	10	47	4	0
4	1	16	4	0	8	0	32	0	0	11	11	47	8	0
4	2	16	8	0	8	1	32	4	0	12	0	48	0	0
4	3	17	0	0	8	2	32	8	0	12	1	48	4	0
4	4	17	4	0	8	3	33	0	0	12	2	48	8	0
4	5	17	8	0	8	4	33	4	0	12	3	49	0	0
4	6	18	0	0	8	5	33	8	0	12	4	49	4	0
4	7	18	4	0	8	6	34	0	0	12	5	49	8	0
4	8	18	8	0	8	7	34	4	0	12	6	50	0	0
4	9	19	0	0	8	8	34	8	0	12	7	50	4	0
4	10	19	4	0	8	9	35	0	0	12	8	50	8	0
4	11	19	8	0	8	10	35	4	0	12	9	51	0	0
5	0	20	0	0	8	11	35	8	0	12	10	51	4	0
5	1	20	4	0	9	0	36	0	0	12	11	51	8	0
5	2	20	8	0	9	1	36	4	0	13	0	52	0	0
5	3	21	0	0	9	2	36	8	0					
5	4	21	4	0	9	3	37	0	0					

WITH STRIPED HOLLAND.

4-ft. 1-in.

4-ft. 1-in. by				4-ft. 1-in. by				4-ft. 1-in. by			
ft. in.	ft.	in.	pts.	ft. in.	ft.	in.	pts.	ft. in.	ft.	in.	pts.
1 6	= 6	1	6	5 5	=22	1	5	9 4	=38	1	4
1 7	6	5	7	5 6	22	5	6	9 5	38	5	5
1 8	6	9	8	5 7	22	9	7	9 6	38	9	6
1 9	7	1	9	5 8	23	1	8	9 7	39	1	7
1 10	7	5	10	5 9	23	5	9	9 8	39	5	8
1 11	7	9	11	5 10	23	9	10	9 9	39	9	9
2 0	8	2	0	5 11	24	1	11	9 10	40	1	10
2 1	8	6	1	6 0	24	6	0	9 11	40	5	11
2 2	8	10	2	6 1	24	10	1	10 0	40	10	0
2 3	9	2	3	6 2	25	2	2	10 1	41	2	1
2 4	9	6	4	6 3	25	6	3	10 2	41	6	2
2 5	9	10	5	6 4	25	10	4	10 3	41	10	3
2 6	10	2	6	6 5	26	2	5	10 4	42	2	4
2 7	10	6	7	6 6	26	6	6	10 5	42	6	5
2 8	10	10	8	6 7	26	10	7	10 6	42	10	6
2 9	11	2	9	6 8	27	2	8	10 7	43	2	7
2 10	11	6	10	6 9	27	6	9	10 8	43	6	8
2 11	11	10	11	6 10	27	10	10	10 9	43	10	9
3 0	12	3	0	6 11	28	2	11	10 10	44	2	10
3 1	12	7	1	7 0	28	7	0	10 11	44	6	11
3 2	12	11	2	7 1	28	11	1	11 0	44	11	0
3 3	13	3	3	7 2	29	3	2	11 1	45	3	1
3 4	13	7	4	7 3	29	7	3	11 2	45	7	2
3 5	13	11	5	7 4	29	11	4	11 3	45	11	3
3 6	14	3	6	7 5	30	3	5	11 4	46	3	4
3 7	14	7	7	7 6	30	7	6	11 5	46	7	5
3 8	14	11	8	7 7	30	11	7	11 6	46	11	6
3 9	15	3	9	7 8	31	3	8	11 7	47	3	7
3 10	15	7	10	7 9	31	7	9	11 8	47	7	8
3 11	15	11	11	7 10	31	11	10	11 9	47	11	9
4 0	16	4	0	7 11	32	3	11	11 10	48	3	10
4 1	16	8	1	8 0	32	8	0	11 11	48	7	11
4 2	17	0	2	8 1	33	0	1	12 0	49	0	0
4 3	17	4	3	8 2	33	4	2	12 1	49	4	1
4 4	17	8	4	8 3	33	8	3	12 2	49	8	2
4 5	18	0	5	8 4	34	0	4	12 3	50	0	3
4 6	18	4	6	8 5	34	4	5	12 4	50	4	4
4 7	18	8	7	8 6	34	8	6	12 5	50	8	5
4 8	19	0	8	8 7	35	0	7	12 6	51	0	6
4 9	19	4	9	8 8	35	4	8	12 7	51	4	7
4 10	19	8	10	8 9	35	8	9	12 8	51	8	8
4 11	20	0	11	8 10	36	0	10	12 9	52	0	9
5 0	20	5	0	8 11	36	4	11	12 10	52	4	10
5 1	20	9	1	9 0	36	9	0	12 11	52	8	11
5 2	21	1	2	9 1	37	1	1	13 0	53	1	0
5 3	21	5	3	9 2	37	5	2				
5 4	21	9	4	9 3	37	9	3				

ROLLER BLINDS ON AN IMPROVED PRINCIPLE

4-ft. 2-in.

4-ft. 2-in. by			4-ft. 2-in by			4-ft. 2-in. by		
ft. in.	ft.	in. pts.	ft. in.	ft.	in. pts.	ft. in.	ft.	in. pts.
1 6	= 6	3 0	5 5	=22	6 10	9 4	=38	10 8
1 7	6	7 2	5 6	22	11 0	9 5	39	2 10
1 8	6	11 4	5 7	23	3 2	9 6	39	7 0
1 9	7	3 6	5 8	23	7 4	9 7	39	11 2
1 10	7	7 8	5 9	23	11 6	9 8	40	3 4
1 11	7	11 10	5 10	24	3 8	9 9	40	7 6
2 0	8	4 0	5 11	24	7 10	9 10	40	11 8
2 1	8	8 2	6 0	25	0 0	9 11	41	3 10
2 2	9	0 4	6 1	25	4 2	10 0	41	8 0
2 3	9	4 6	6 2	25	8 4	10 1	42	0 2
2 4	9	8 8	6 3	26	0 6	10 2	42	4 4
2 5	10	0 10	6 4	26	4 8	10 3	42	8 6
2 6	10	5 0	6 5	26	8 10	10 4	43	0 8
2 7	10	9 2	6 6	27	1 0	10 5	43	4 10
2 8	11	1 4	6 7	27	5 2	10 6	43	9 0
2 9	11	5 6	6 8	27	9 4	10 7	44	1 2
2 10	11	9 8	6 9	28	1 6	10 8	44	5 4
2 11	12	1 10	6 10	28	5 8	10 9	44	9 6
3 0	12	6 0	6 11	28	9 10	10 10	45	1 8
3 1	12	10 2	7 0	29	2 0	10 11	45	5 10
3 2	13	2 4	7 1	29	6 2	11 0	45	10 0
3 3	13	6 6	7 2	29	10 4	11 1	46	2 2
3 4	13	10 8	7 3	30	2 6	11 2	46	6 4
3 5	14	2 10	7 4	30	6 8	11 3	46	10 6
3 6	14	7 0	7 5	30	10 10	11 4	47	2 8
3 7	14	11 2	7 6	31	3 0	11 5	47	6 10
3 8	15	3 4	7 7	31	7 2	11 6	47	11 0
3 9	15	7 6	7 8	31	11 4	11 7	48	3 2
3 10	15	11 8	7 9	32	3 6	11 8	48	7 4
3 11	16	3 10	7 10	32	7 8	11 9	48	11 6
4 0	16	8 0	7 11	32	11 10	11 10	49	3 8
4 1	17	0 2	8 0	33	4 0	11 11	49	7 10
4 2	17	4 4	8 1	33	8 2	12 0	50	0 0
4 3	17	8 6	8 2	34	0 4	12 1	50	4 2
4 4	18	0 8	8 3	34	4 6	12 2	50	8 4
4 5	18	4 10	8 4	34	8 8	12 3	51	0 6
4 6	18	9 0	8 5	35	0 10	12 4	51	4 8
4 7	19	1 2	8 6	35	5 0	12 5	51	8 10
4 8	19	5 4	8 7	35	9 2	12 6	52	1 0
4 9	19	9 6	8 8	36	1 4	12 7	52	5 2
4 10	20	1 8	8 9	36	5 6	12 8	52	9 4
4 11	20	5 10	8 10	36	9 8	12 9	53	1 6
5 0	20	10 0	8 11	37	1 10	12 10	53	5 8
5 1	21	2 2	9 0	37	6 0	12 11	53	9 10
5 2	21	6 4	9 1	37	10 2	13 0	54	2 0
5 3	21	10 6	9 2	38	2 4			
5 4	22	2 8	9 3	38	6 6			

FOR SCHOOLS AND PUBLIC BUILDINGS.

4-ft. 3-in.

4-ft. 3-in. by				4-ft. 3-in. by				4-ft. 3-in. by			
ft. in.	ft.	in.	pts.	t. in.	ft.	in.	pts.	ft. in.	ft.	in.	pts.
1 6	= 6	4	6	5 5	= 23	0	3	9 4	= 39	8	0
1 7	6	8	9	5 6	23	4	6	9 5	40	0	3
1 8	7	1	0	5 7	23	8	9	9 6	40	4	6
1 9	7	5	3	5 8	24	1	0	9 7	40	8	9
1 10	7	9	6	5 9	24	5	3	9 8	41	1	0
1 11	8	1	9	5 10	24	9	6	9 9	41	5	3
2 0	8	6	0	5 11	25	1	9	9 10	41	9	6
2 1	8	10	3	6 0	25	6	0	9 11	42	1	9
2 2	9	2	6	6 1	25	10	3	10 0	42	6	0
2 3	9	6	9	6 2	26	2	6	10 1	42	10	3
2 4	9	11	0	6 3	26	6	9	10 2	43	2	6
2 5	10	3	3	6 4	26	11	0	10 3	43	6	9
2 6	10	7	6	6 5	27	3	3	10 4	43	11	0
2 7	10	11	9	6 6	27	7	6	10 5	44	3	3
2 8	11	4	0	6 7	27	11	9	10 6	44	7	6
2 9	11	8	3	6 8	28	4	0	10 7	44	11	9
2 10	12	0	6	6 9	28	8	3	10 8	45	4	0
2 11	12	4	9	6 10	29	0	6	10 9	45	8	3
3 0	12	9	0	6 11	29	4	9	10 10	46	0	6
3 1	13	1	3	7 0	29	9	0	10 11	46	4	9
3 2	13	5	6	7 1	30	1	3	11 0	46	9	0
3 3	13	9	9	7 2	30	5	6	11 1	47	1	3
3 4	14	2	0	7 3	30	9	9	11 2	47	5	6
3 5	14	6	3	7 4	31	2	0	11 3	47	9	9
3 6	14	10	6	7 5	31	6	3	11 4	48	2	0
3 7	15	2	9	7 6	31	10	6	11 5	48	6	3
3 8	15	7	0	7 7	32	2	9	11 6	48	10	6
3 9	15	11	3	7 8	32	7	0	11 7	49	2	9
3 10	16	3	6	7 9	32	11	3	11 8	49	7	0
3 11	16	7	9	7 10	33	3	6	11 9	49	11	3
4 0	17	0	0	7 11	33	7	9	11 10	50	3	6
4 1	17	4	3	8 0	34	0	0	11 11	50	7	9
4 2	17	8	6	8 1	34	4	3	12 0	51	0	0
4 3	18	0	9	8 2	34	8	6	12 1	51	4	3
4 4	18	5	0	8 3	35	0	9	12 2	51	8	6
4 5	18	9	3	8 4	35	5	0	12 3	52	0	9
4 6	19	1	6	8 5	35	9	3	12 4	52	5	0
4 7	19	5	9	8 6	36	1	6	12 5	52	9	3
4 8	19	10	0	8 7	36	5	9	12 6	53	1	6
4 9	20	2	3	8 8	36	10	0	12 7	53	5	9
4 10	20	6	6	8 9	37	2	3	12 8	53	10	0
4 11	20	10	9	8 10	37	6	6	12 9	54	2	3
5 0	21	3	0	8 11	37	10	9	12 10	54	6	6
5 1	21	7	3	9 0	38	3	0	12 11	54	10	9
5 2	21	11	6	9 1	38	7	3	13 0	55	3	0
5 3	22	3	9	9 2	38	11	6				
5 4	22	8	0	9 3	39	3	9				

36, FARRINGDON STREET, LONDON, E.C.

4-ft. 4-in.

4-ft. 4-in. by				4-ft. 4-in. by				4-ft. 4-in. by			
ft. in.	ft.	in.	pts.	ft. in.	ft.	in.	pts.	ft. in.	ft.	in.	pts.
1 6	= 6	6	0	5 5	=23	5	8	9 4	=40	5	4
1 7	6	10	4	5 6	23	10	0	9 5	40	9	8
1 8	7	2	8	5 7	24	2	4	9 6	41	2	0
1 9	7	7	0	5 8	24	6	8	9 7	41	6	4
1 10	7	11	4	5 9	24	11	0	9 8	41	10	8
1 11	8	3	8	5 10	25	3	4	9 9	42	3	0
2 0	8	8	0	5 11	25	7	8	9 10	42	7	4
2 1	9	0	4	6 0	26	0	0	9 11	42	11	8
2 2	9	4	8	6 1	26	4	4	10 0	43	4	0
2 3	9	9	0	6 2	26	8	8	10 1	43	8	4
2 4	10	1	4	6 3	27	1	0	10 2	44	0	8
2 5	10	5	8	6 4	27	5	4	10 3	44	5	0
2 6	10	10	0	6 5	27	9	8	10 4	44	9	4
2 7	11	2	4	6 6	28	2	0	10 5	45	1	8
2 8	11	6	8	6 7	28	6	4	10 6	45	6	0
2 9	11	11	0	6 8	28	10	8	10 7	45	10	4
2 10	12	3	4	6 9	29	3	0	10 8	46	2	8
2 11	12	7	8	6 10	29	7	4	10 9	46	7	0
3 0	13	0	0	6 11	29	11	8	10 10	46	11	4
3 1	13	4	4	7 0	30	4	0	10 11	47	3	8
3 2	13	8	8	7 1	30	8	4	11 0	47	8	0
3 3	14	1	0	7 2	31	0	8	11 1	48	0	4
3 4	14	5	4	7 3	31	5	0	11 2	48	4	8
3 5	14	9	8	7 4	31	9	4	11 3	48	9	0
3 6	15	2	0	7 5	32	1	8	11 4	49	1	4
3 7	15	6	4	7 6	32	6	0	11 5	49	5	8
3 8	15	10	8	7 7	32	10	4	11 6	49	10	0
3 9	16	3	0	7 8	33	2	8	11 7	50	2	4
3 10	16	7	4	7 9	33	7	0	11 8	50	6	8
3 11	16	11	8	7 10	33	11	4	11 9	50	11	0
4 0	17	4	0	7 11	34	3	8	11 10	51	3	4
4 1	17	8	4	8 0	34	8	0	11 11	51	7	8
4 2	18	0	8	8 1	35	0	4	12 0	52	0	0
4 3	18	5	0	8 2	35	4	8	12 1	52	4	4
4 4	18	9	4	8 3	35	9	0	12 2	52	8	8
4 5	19	1	8	8 4	36	1	4	12 3	53	1	0
4 6	19	6	0	8 5	36	5	8	12 4	53	5	4
4 7	19	10	4	8 6	36	10	0	12 5	53	9	8
4 8	20	2	8	8 7	37	2	4	12 6	54	2	0
4 9	20	7	0	8 8	37	6	8	12 7	54	6	4
4 10	20	11	4	8 9	37	11	0	12 8	54	10	8
4 11	21	3	8	8 10	38	3	4	12 9	55	3	0
5 0	21	8	0	8 11	38	7	8	12 10	55	7	4
5 1	22	0	4	9 0	39	0	0	12 11	55	11	8
5 2	22	4	8	9 1	39	4	4	13 0	56	4	0
5 3	22	9	0	9 2	39	8	8				
5 4	23	1	4	9 3	40	1	0				

OF SILK OR MUSLIN.

4-ft. 5-in.

4-ft. 5-in. by				4-ft. 5-in. by				4-ft. 5-in. by			
ft. in.	ft.	in.	pts.	ft. in.	ft.	in.	pts.	ft. in.	ft.	in.	pts.
1 6	= 6	7	6	5 5	=23	11	1	9 4	=41	2	8
1 7	6	11	11	5 6	24	3	6	9 5	41	7	1
1 8	7	4	4	5 7	24	7	11	9 6	41	11	6
1 9	7	8	9	5 8	25	0	4	9 7	42	3	11
1 10	8	1	2	5 9	25	4	9	9 8	42	8	4
1 11	8	5	7	5 10	25	9	2	9 9	43	0	9
2 0	8	10	0	5 11	26	1	7	9 10	43	5	2
2 1	9	2	5	6 0	26	6	0	9 11	43	9	7
2 2	9	6	10	6 1	26	10	5	10 0	44	2	0
2 3	9	11	3	6 2	27	2	10	10 1	44	6	5
2 4	10	3	8	6 3	27	7	3	10 2	44	10	10
2 5	10	8	1	6 4	27	11	8	10 3	45	3	3
2 6	11	0	6	6 5	28	4	1	10 4	45	7	8
2 7	11	4	11	6 6	28	8	6	10 5	46	0	1
2 8	11	9	4	6 7	29	0	11	10 6	46	4	6
2 9	12	1	9	6 8	29	5	4	10 7	46	8	11
2 10	12	6	2	6 9	29	9	9	10 8	47	1	4
2 11	12	10	7	6 10	30	2	2	10 9	47	5	9
3 0	13	3	0	6 11	30	6	7	10 10	47	10	2
3 1	13	7	5	7 0	30	11	0	10 11	48	2	7
3 2	13	11	10	7 1	31	3	5	11 0	48	7	0
3 3	14	4	3	7 2	31	7	10	11 1	48	11	5
3 4	14	8	8	7 3	32	0	3	11 2	49	3	10
3 5	15	1	1	7 4	32	4	8	11 3	49	8	3
3 6	15	5	6	7 5	32	9	1	11 4	50	0	8
3 7	15	9	11	7 6	33	1	6	11 5	50	5	1
3 8	16	2	4	7 7	33	5	11	11 6	50	9	6
3 9	16	6	9	7 8	33	10	4	11 7	51	1	11
3 10	16	11	2	7 9	34	2	9	11 8	51	6	4
3 11	17	3	7	7 10	34	7	2	11 9	51	10	9
4 0	17	8	0	7 11	34	11	7	11 10	52	3	2
4 1	18	0	5	8 0	35	4	0	11 11	52	7	7
4 2	18	4	10	8 1	35	8	5	12 0	53	0	0
4 3	18	9	3	8 2	36	0	10	12 1	53	4	5
4 4	19	1	8	8 3	36	5	3	12 2	53	8	10
4 5	19	6	1	8 4	36	9	8	12 3	54	1	3
4 6	19	10	6	8 5	37	2	1	12 4	54	5	8
4 7	20	2	11	8 6	37	6	6	12 5	54	10	1
4 8	20	7	4	8 7	37	10	11	12 6	55	2	6
4 9	20	11	9	8 8	38	3	4	12 7	55	6	11
4 10	21	4	2	8 9	38	7	9	12 8	55	11	4
4 11	21	8	7	8 10	39	0	2	12 9	56	3	9
5 0	22	1	0	8 11	39	4	7	12 10	56	8	2
5 1	22	5	5	9 0	39	9	0	12 11	57	0	7
5 2	22	9	10	9 1	40	1	5	13 0	57	5	0
5 3	23	2	3	9 2	40	5	10				
5 4	23	6	8	9 3	40	10	3				

4-ft. 6-in.

4-ft. 6-in. by				4-ft. 6-in. by				4-ft. 6-in. by		
ft. in.	ft.	in.	pts.	ft. in.	ft.	in.	pts.	ft. in.	ft.	in.	pts.
1 6	= 6	9	0	5 5	=24	4	6	9 4	=42	0	0
1 7	7	1	6	5 6	24	9	0	9 5	42	4	6
1 8	7	6	0	5 7	25	1	6	9 6	42	9	0
1 9	7	10	6	5 8	25	6	0	9 7	43	1	6
1 10	8	3	0	5 9	25	10	6	9 8	43	6	0
1 11	8	7	6	5 10	26	3	0	9 9	43	10	6
2 0	9	0	0	5 11	26	7	6	9 10	44	3	0
2 1	9	4	6	6 0	27	0	0	9 11	44	7	6
2 2	9	9	0	6 1	27	4	6	10 0	45	0	0
2 3	10	1	6	6 2	27	9	0	10 1	45	4	6
2 4	10	6	0	6 3	28	1	6	10 2	45	9	0
2 5	10	10	6	6 4	28	6	0	10 3	46	1	6
2 6	11	3	0	6 5	28	10	6	10 4	46	6	0
2 7	11	7	6	6 6	29	3	0	10 5	46	10	6
2 8	12	0	0	6 7	29	7	6	10 6	47	3	0
2 9	12	4	6	6 8	30	0	0	10 7	47	7	6
2 10	12	9	0	6 9	30	4	6	10 8	48	0	0
2 11	13	1	6	6 10	30	9	0	10 9	48	4	6
3 0	13	6	0	6 11	31	1	6	10 10	48	9	0
3 1	13	10	6	7 0	31	6	0	10 11	49	1	6
3 2	14	3	0	7 1	31	10	6	11 0	49	6	0
3 3	14	7	6	7 2	32	3	0	11 1	49	10	6
3 4	15	0	0	7 3	32	7	6	11 2	50	3	0
3 5	15	4	6	7 4	33	0	0	11 3	50	7	6
3 6	15	9	0	7 5	33	4	6	11 4	51	0	0
3 7	16	1	6	7 6	33	9	0	11 5	51	4	6
3 8	16	6	0	7 7	34	1	6	11 6	51	9	0
3 9	16	10	6	7 8	34	6	0	11 7	52	1	6
3 10	17	3	0	7 9	34	10	6	11 8	52	6	0
3 11	17	7	6	7 10	35	3	0	11 9	52	10	6
4 0	18	0	0	7 11	35	7	6	11 10	53	3	0
4 1	18	4	6	8 0	36	0	0	11 11	53	7	6
4 2	18	9	0	8 1	36	4	6	12 0	54	0	0
4 3	19	1	6	8 2	36	9	0	12 1	54	4	6
4 4	19	6	0	8 3	37	1	6	12 2	54	9	0
4 5	19	10	6	8 4	37	6	0	12 3	55	1	6
4 6	20	3	0	8 5	37	10	6	12 4	55	6	0
4 7	20	7	6	8 6	38	3	0	12 5	55	10	6
4 8	21	0	0	8 7	38	7	6	12 6	56	3	0
4 9	21	4	6	8 8	39	0	0	12 7	56	7	6
4 10	21	9	0	8 9	39	4	6	12 8	57	0	0
4 11	22	1	6	8 10	39	9	0	12 9	57	4	6
5 0	22	6	0	8 11	40	1	6	12 10	57	9	0
5 1	22	10	6	9 0	40	6	0	12 11	58	1	6
5 2	23	3	0	9 1	40	10	6	13 0	58	6	0
5 3	23	7	6	9 2	41	3	0				
5 4	24	0	0	9 3	41	7	6				

WITH METAL TUBE TOP RAILS.

4-ft. 7-in.

4-ft. 7-in. by			4-ft. 7-in. by			4-ft. 7-in. by		
ft. in.	ft. in.	pts.	ft. in.	ft. in.	pts.	ft. in.	ft. in.	pts.
1 6	= 6 10	6	5 5	=24 9	11	9 4	=42 9	4
1 7	7 3	1	5 6	25 2	6	9 5	43 1	11
1 8	7 7	8	5 7	25 7	1	9 6	43 6	6
1 9	8 0	3	5 8	25 11	8	9 7	43 11	1
1 10	8 4	10	5 9	26 4	3	9 8	44 3	8
1 11	8 9	5	5 10	26 8	10	9 9	44 8	3
2 0	9 2	0	5 11	27 1	5	9 10	45 0	10
2 1	9 6	7	6 0	27 6	0	9 11	45 5	3
2 2	9 11	2	6 1	27 10	7	10 0	45 10	0
2 3	10 3	9	6 2	28 3	2	10 1	46 2	7
2 4	10 8	4	6 3	28 7	9	10 2	46 7	2
2 5	11 0	11	6 4	29 0	4	10 3	46 11	9
2 6	11 5	6	6 5	29 4	11	10 4	47 4	4
2 7	11 10	1	6 6	29 9	6	10 5	47 8	11
2 8	12 2	8	6 7	30 2	1	10 6	48 1	6
2 9	12 7	3	6 8	30 6	8	10 7	48 6	1
2 10	12 11	10	6 9	30 11	3	10 8	48 10	8
2 11	13 4	5	6 10	31 3	10	10 9	49 3	3
3 0	13 9	0	6 11	31 8	5	10 10	49 7	10
3 1	14 1	7	7 0	32 1	0	10 11	50 0	5
3 2	14 6	2	7 1	32 5	7	11 0	50 5	0
3 3	14 10	9	7 2	32 10	2	11 1	50 9	7
3 4	15 3	4	7 3	33 2	9	11 2	51 2	2
3 5	15 7	11	7 4	33 7	4	11 3	51 6	9
3 6	16 0	6	7 5	33 11	11	11 4	51 11	4
3 7	16 5	1	7 6	34 4	6	11 5	52 3	11
3 8	16 9	8	7 7	34 9	1	11 6	52 8	6
3 9	17 2	3	7 8	35 1	8	11 7	53 1	1
3 10	17 6	10	7 9	35 6	3	11 8	53 5	8
3 11	17 11	5	7 10	35 10	10	11 9	53 10	3
4 0	18 4	0	7 11	36 3	5	11 10	54 2	10
4 1	18 8	7	8 0	36 8	0	11 11	54 7	5
4 2	19 1	2	8 1	37 0	7	12 0	55 0	0
4 3	19 5	9	8 2	37 5	2	12 1	55 4	7
4 4	19 10	4	8 3	37 9	9	12 2	55 9	2
4 5	20 2	11	8 4	38 2	4	12 3	56 1	9
4 6	20 7	6	8 5	38 6	11	12 4	56 6	4
4 7	21 0	1	8 6	38 11	6	12 5	56 10	11
4 8	21 4	8	8 7	39 4	1	12 6	57 3	6
4 9	21 9	3	8 8	39 8	8	12 7	57 8	1
4 10	22 1	10	8 9	40 1	3	12 8	58 0	8
4 11	22 6	5	8 10	40 5	10	12 9	58 5	3
5 0	22 11	0	8 11	40 10	5	12 10	58 9	10
5 1	23 3	7	9 0	41 3	0	12 11	59 2	5
5 2	23 8	2	9 1	41 7	7	13 0	59 7	0
5 3	24 0	9	9 2	42 0	2			
5 4	24 5	4	9 3	42 4	9			

4-ft. 8-in.

4-ft. 8-in. by

ft. in.	ft. in. pts.
1 6	= 7 0 0
1 7	7 4 8
1 8	7 9 4
1 9	8 2 0
1 10	8 6 8
1 11	8 11 4
2 0	9 4 0
2 1	9 8 8
2 2	10 1 4
2 3	10 6 0
2 4	10 10 8
2 5	11 3 4
2 6	11 8 0
2 7	12 0 8
2 8	12 5 4
2 9	12 10 0
2 10	13 2 8
2 11	13 7 4
3 0	14 0 0
3 1	14 4 8
3 2	14 9 4
3 3	15 2 0
3 4	15 6 8
3 5	15 11 4
3 6	16 4 0
3 7	16 8 8
3 8	17 1 4
3 9	17 6 0
3 10	17 10 8
3 11	18 3 4
4 0	18 8 0
4 1	19 0 8
4 2	19 5 4
4 3	19 10 0
4 4	20 2 8
4 5	20 7 4
4 6	21 0 0
4 7	21 4 8
4 8	21 9 4
4 9	22 2 0
4 10	22 6 8
4 11	22 11 4
5 0	23 4 0
5 1	23 8 8
5 2	24 1 4
5 3	24 6 0
5 4	24 10 8

4-ft. 8-in. by

ft. in.	ft. iu. pts.
5 5	=25 3 4
5 6	25 8 0
5 7	26 0 8
5 8	26 5 4
5 9	26 10 0
5 10	27 2 8
5 11	27 7 4
6 0	28 0 0
6 1	28 4 8
6 2	28 9 4
6 3	29 2 0
6 4	29 6 8
6 5	29 11 4
6 6	30 4 0
6 7	30 8 8
6 8	31 1 4
6 9	31 6 0
6 10	31 10 8
6 11	32 3 4
7 0	32 8 0
7 1	33 0 8
7 2	33 5 4
7 3	33 10 0
7 4	34 2 8
7 5	34 7 4
7 6	35 0 0
7 7	35 4 8
7 8	35 9 4
7 9	36 2 0
7 10	36 6 8
7 11	36 11 4
8 0	37 4 0
8 1	37 8 8
8 2	38 1 4
8 3	38 6 0
8 4	38 10 8
8 5	39 3 4
8 6	39 8 0
8 7	40 0 8
8 8	40 5 4
8 9	40 10 0
8 10	41 2 8
8 11	41 7 4
9 0	42 0 0
9 1	42 4 8
9 2	42 9 4
9 3	43 2 0

4-ft. 8-in. by

ft. in.	ft. in. pts.
9 4	=43 6 8
9 5	43 11 4
9 6	44 4 0
9 7	44 8 8
9 8	45 1 4
9 9	45 6 0
9 10	45 10 8
9 11	46 3 4
10 0	46 8 0
10 1	47 0 8
10 2	47 5 4
10 3	47 10 0
10 4	48 2 8
10 5	48 7 4
10 6	49 0 0
10 7	49 4 8
10 8	49 9 4
10 9	50 2 0
10 10	50 6 8
10 11	50 11 4
11 0	51 4 0
11 1	51 8 8
11 2	52 1 4
11 3	52 6 0
11 4	52 10 8
11 5	53 3 4
11 6	53 8 0
11 7	54 0 8
11 8	54 5 4
11 9	54 10 0
11 10	55 2 8
11 11	55 7 4
12 0	56 0 0
12 1	56 4 8
12 2	56 9 4
12 3	57 2 0
12 4	57 6 8
12 5	57 11 4
12 6	58 4 0
12 7	58 8 8
12 8	59 1 4
12 9	59 6 0
12 10	59 10 8
12 11	60 3 4
13 0	60 8 0

FOR CASEMENT WINDOWS.

4-ft. 9-in.

4-ft. 9-in. by			4-ft. 9-in. by			4-ft. 9-in. by		
ft. in.	ft. in. pts.		ft. in.	ft. in. pts.		ft. in.	ft. in. pts.	
1 6	= 7 1 6		5 5	=25 8 9		9 4	=44 4 0	
1 7	7 6 3		5 6	26 1 6		9 5	44 8 9	
1 8	7 11 0		5 7	26 6 3		9 6	45 1 6	
1 9	8 3 9		5 8	26 11 0		9 7	45 6 3	
1 10	8 8 6		5 9	27 3 9		9 8	45 11 0	
1 11	9 1 3		5 10	27 8 6		9 9	46 3 9	
2 0	9 6 0		5 11	28 1 3		9 10	46 8 6	
2 1	9 10 9		6 0	28 6 0		9 11	47 1 3	
2 2	10 3 6		6 1	28 10 9		10 0	47 6 0	
2 3	10 8 3		6 2	29 3 6		10 1	47 10 9	
2 4	11 1 0		6 3	29 8 3		10 2	48 3 6	
2 5	11 5 9		6 4	30 1 0		10 3	48 8 3	
2 6	11 10 6		6 5	30 5 9		10 4	49 1 0	
2 7	12 3 3		6 6	30 10 6		10 5	49 5 9	
2 8	12 8 0		6 7	31 3 3		10 6	49 10 6	
2 9	13 0 9		6 8	31 8 0		10 7	50 3 3	
2 10	13 5 6		6 9	32 0 9		10 8	50 8 0	
2 11	13 10 3		6 10	32 5 6		10 9	51 0 9	
3 0	14 3 0		6 11	32 10 3		10 10	51 5 6	
3 1	14 7 9		7 0	33 3 0		10 11	51 10 3	
3 2	15 0 6		7 1	33 7 9		11 0	52 3 0	
3 3	15 5 3		7 2	34 0 6		11 1	52 7 9	
3 4	15 10 0		7 3	34 5 3		11 2	53 0 6	
3 5	16 2 9		7 4	34 10 0		11 3	53 5 3	
3 6	16 7 6		7 5	35 2 9		11 4	53 10 0	
3 7	17 0 3		7 6	35 7 6		11 5	54 2 9	
3 8	17 5 0		7 7	36 0 3		11 6	54 7 6	
3 9	17 9 9		7 8	36 5 0		11 7	55 0 3	
3 10	18 2 6		7 9	36 9 9		11 8	55 5 0	
3 11	18 7 3		7 10	37 2 6		11 9	55 9 9	
4 0	19 0 0		7 11	37 7 3		11 10	56 2 6	
4 1	19 4 9		8 0	38 0 0		11 11	56 7 3	
4 2	19 9 6		8 1	38 4 9		12 0	57 0 0	
4 3	20 2 3		8 2	38 9 6		12 1	57 4 9	
4 4	20 7 0		8 3	39 2 3		12 2	57 9 6	
4 5	20 11 9		8 4	39 7 0		12 3	58 2 3	
4 6	21 4 6		8 5	39 11 9		12 4	58 7 0	
4 7	21 9 3		8 6	40 4 6		12 5	58 11 9	
4 8	22 2 0		8 7	40 9 3		12 6	59 4 6	
4 9	22 6 9		8 8	41 2 0		12 7	59 9 3	
4 10	22 11 6		8 9	41 6 9		12 8	60 2 0	
4 11	23 4 3		8 10	41 11 6		12 9	60 6 9	
5 0	23 9 0		8 11	42 4 3		12 10	60 11 6	
5 1	24 1 9		9 0	42 9 0		12 11	61 4 3	
5 2	24 6 6		9 1	43 1 9		13 0	61 9 0	
5 3	24 11 3		9 2	43 6 6				
5 4	25 4 0		9 3	43 11 3				

4-ft. 10-in.

4-ft. 10-in. by					4-ft. 10-in. by					4-ft. 10-in. by			
ft.	in.	ft.	in.	pts.	ft.	in.	ft.	in.	pts.	ft.	in.	ft.	in.	pts.
1	6	= 7	3	0	5	5	=26	2	2	9	4	=45	1	4
1	7	7	7	10	5	6	26	7	0	9	5	45	6	2
1	8	8	0	8	5	7	26	11	10	9	6	45	11	0
1	9	8	5	6	5	8	27	4	8	9	7	46	3	10
1	10	8	10	4	5	9	27	9	6	9	8	46	8	8
1	11	9	3	2	5	10	28	2	4	9	9	47	1	6
2	0	9	8	0	5	11	28	7	2	9	10	47	6	4
2	1	10	0	10	6	0	29	0	0	9	11	47	11	2
2	2	10	5	8	6	1	29	4	10	10	0	48	4	0
2	3	10	10	6	6	2	29	9	8	10	1	48	8	10
2	4	11	3	4	6	3	30	2	6	10	2	49	1	8
2	5	11	8	2	6	4	30	7	4	10	3	49	6	6
2	6	12	1	0	6	5	31	0	2	10	4	49	11	4
2	7	12	5	10	6	6	31	5	0	10	5	50	4	2
2	8	12	10	8	6	7	31	9	10	10	6	50	9	0
2	9	13	3	6	6	8	32	2	8	10	7	51	1	10
2	10	13	8	4	6	9	32	7	6	10	8	51	6	8
2	11	14	1	2	6	10	33	0	4	10	9	51	11	6
3	0	14	6	0	6	11	33	5	2	10	10	52	4	4
3	1	14	10	10	7	0	33	10	0	10	11	52	9	2
3	2	15	3	8	7	1	34	2	10	11	0	53	2	0
3	3	15	8	6	7	2	34	7	8	11	1	53	6	10
3	4	16	1	4	7	3	35	0	6	11	2	53	11	8
3	5	16	6	2	7	4	35	5	4	11	3	54	4	6
3	6	16	11	0	7	5	35	10	2	11	4	54	9	4
3	7	17	3	10	7	6	36	3	0	11	5	55	2	2
3	8	17	8	8	7	7	36	7	10	11	6	55	7	0
3	9	18	1	6	7	8	37	0	8	11	7	55	11	10
3	10	18	6	4	7	9	37	5	6	11	8	56	4	8
3	11	18	11	2	7	10	37	10	4	11	9	56	9	6
4	0	19	4	0	7	11	38	3	2	11	10	57	2	4
4	1	19	8	10	8	0	38	8	0	11	11	57	7	2
4	2	20	1	8	8	1	39	0	10	12	0	58	0	0
4	3	20	6	6	8	2	39	5	8	12	1	58	4	10
4	4	20	11	4	8	3	39	10	6	12	2	58	9	8
4	5	21	4	2	8	4	40	3	4	12	3	59	2	6
4	6	21	9	0	8	5	40	8	2	12	4	59	7	4
4	7	22	1	10	8	6	41	1	0	12	5	60	0	2
4	8	22	6	8	8	7	41	5	10	12	6	60	5	0
4	9	22	11	6	8	8	41	10	8	12	7	60	9	10
4	10	23	4	4	8	9	42	3	6	12	8	61	2	8
4	11	23	9	2	8	10	42	8	4	12	9	61	7	6
5	0	24	2	0	8	11	43	1	2	12	10	62	0	4
5	1	24	6	10	9	0	43	6	0	12	11	62	5	2
5	2	24	11	8	9	1	43	10	10	13	0	62	10	0
5	3	25	4	6	9	2	44	3	8					
5	4	25	9	4	9	3	44	8	6					

WITH METAL TUBE SLIDES.

4-ft. 11-in.

4-ft. 11-in. by				4-ft. 11-in. by				4-ft. 11-in. by			
ft.	in.	ft.	in. pts.	ft.	in.	ft.	in. pts.	ft.	in.	ft.	in. pts.
1	6	= 7	4 .6	5	5	=26	7 7	9	4	=45	10 8
1	7	7	9 5	5	6	27	0 6	9	5	46	3 7
1	8	8	2 4	5	7	27	5 5	9	6	46	8 6
1	9	8	7 3	5	8	27	10 4	9	7	47	1 5
1	10	9	0 2	5	9	28	3 3	9	8	47	6 4
1	11	9	5 1	5	10	28	8 2	9	9	47	11 3
2	0	9	10 0	5	11	29	1 1	9	10	48	4 2
2	1	10	2 11	6	0	29	6 0	9	11	48	9 1
2	2	10	7 10	6	1	29	10 11	10	0	49	2 0
2	3	11	0 9	6	2	30	3 10	10	1	49	6 11
2	4	11	5 8	6	3	30	8 9	10	2	49	11 10
2	5	11	10 7	6	4	31	1 8	10	3	50	4 9
2	6	12	3 6	6	5	31	6 7	10	4	50	9 8
2	7	12	8 5	6	6	31	11 6	10	5	51	2 7
2	8	13	1 4	6	7	32	4 5	10	6	51	7 6
2	9	13	6 3	6	8	32	9 4	10	7	52	0 5
2	10	13	11 2	6	9	33	2 3	10	8	52	5 4
2	11	14	4 1	6	10	33	7 2	10	9	52	10 3
3	0	14	9 0	6	11	34	0 1	10	10	53	3 2
3	1	15	1 11	7	0	34	5 0	10	11	53	8 1
3	2	15	6 10	7	1	34	9 11	11	0	54	1 0
3	3	15	11 9	7	2	35	2 10	11	1	54	5 11
3	4	16	4 8	7	3	35	7 9	11	2	54	10 10
3	5	16	9 7	7	4	36	0 8	11	3	55	3 9
3	6	17	2 6	7	5	36	5 7	11	4	55	8 8
3	7	17	7 5	7	6	36	10 6	11	5	56	1 7
3	8	18	0 4	7	7	37	3 5	11	6	56	6 6
3	9	18	5 3	7	8	37	8 4	11	7	56	11 5
3	10	18	10 2	7	9	38	1 3	11	8	57	4 4
3	11	19	3 1	7	10	38	6 2	11	9	57	9 3
4	0	19	8 0	7	11	38	11 1	11	10	58	2 2
4	1	20	0 11	8	0	39	4 0	11	11	58	7 1
4	2	20	5 10	8	1	39	8 11	12	0	59	0 0
4	3	20	10 9	8	2	40	1 10	12	1	59	4 11
4	4	21	3 8	8	3	40	6 9	12	2	59	9 10
4	5	21	8 7	8	4	40	11 8	12	3	60	2 9
4	6	22	1 6	8	5	41	4 7	12	4	60	7 8
4	7	22	6 5	8	6	41	9 6	12	5	61	0 7
4	8	22	11 4	8	7	42	2 5	12	6	61	5 6
4	9	23	4 3	8	8	42	7 4	12	7	61	10 5
4	10	23	9 2	8	9	43	0 3	12	8	62	3 4
4	11	24	2 1	8	10	43	5 2	12	9	62	8 3
5	0	24	7 0	8	11	43	10 1	12	10	63	1 2
5	1	24	11 11	9	0	44	3 0	12	11	63	6 1
5	2	25	4 10	9	1	44	7 11	13	0	63	11 0
5	3	25	9 9	9	2	45	0 10				
5	4	26	2 8	9	3	45	5 9				

5-ft.

5-ft. by				5-ft. by				5-ft. by			
ft. in.	ft.	in.	pts.	ft. in.	ft.	in.	pts.	ft. in.	ft.	in.	pts.
1 6	= 7	6	0	5 5	=27	1	0	9 4	=46	8	0
1 7	7	11	0	5 6	27	6	0	9 5	47	1	0
1 8	8	4	0	5 7	27	11	0	9 6	47	6	0
1 9	8	9	0	5 8	28	4	0	9 7	47	11	0
1 10	9	2	0	5 9	28	9	0	9 8	48	4	0
1 11	9	7	0	5 10	29	2	0	9 9	48	9	0
2 0	10	0	0	5 11	29	7	0	9 10	49	2	0
2 1	10	5	0	6 0	30	0	0	9 11	49	7	0
2 2	10	10	0	6 1	30	5	0	10 0	50	0	0
2 3	11	3	0	6 2	30	10	0	10 1	50	5	0
2 4	11	8	0	6 3	31	3	0	10 2	50	10	0
2 5	12	1	0	6 4	31	8	0	10 3	51	3	0
2 6	12	6	0	6 5	32	1	0	10 4	51	8	0
2 7	12	11	0	6 6	32	6	0	10 5	52	1	0
2 8	13	4	0	6 7	32	11	0	10 6	52	6	0
2 9	13	9	0	6 8	33	4	0	10 7	52	11	0
2 10	14	2	0	6 9	33	9	0	10 8	53	4	0
2 11	14	7	0	6 10	34	2	0	10 9	53	9	0
3 0	15	0	0	6 11	34	7	0	10 10	54	2	0
3 1	15	5	0	7 0	35	0	0	10 11	54	7	0
3 2	15	10	0	7 1	35	5	0	11 0	55	0	0
3 3	16	3	0	7 2	35	10	0	11 1	55	5	0
3 4	16	8	0	7 3	36	3	0	11 2	55	10	0
3 5	17	1	0	7 4	36	8	0	11 3	56	3	0
3 6	17	6	0	7 5	37	1	0	11 4	56	8	0
3 7	17	11	0	7 6	37	6	0	11 5	57	1	0
3 8	18	4	0	7 7	37	11	0	11 6	57	6	0
3 9	18	9	0	7 8	38	4	0	11 7	57	11	0
3 10	19	2	0	7 9	38	9	0	11 8	58	4	0
3 11	19	7	0	7 10	39	2	0	11 9	58	9	0
4 0	20	0	0	7 11	39	7	0	11 10	59	2	0
4 1	20	5	0	8 0	40	0	0	11 11	59	7	0
4 2	20	10	0	8 1	40	5	0	12 0	60	0	0
4 3	21	3	0	8 2	40	10	0	12 1	60	5	0
4 4	21	8	0	8 3	41	3	0	12 2	60	10	0
4 5	22	1	0	8 4	41	8	0	12 3	61	3	0
4 6	22	6	0	8 5	42	1	0	12 4	61	8	0
4 7	22	11	0	8 6	42	6	0	12 5	62	1	0
4 8	23	4	0	8 7	42	11	0	12 6	62	6	0
4 9	23	9	0	8 8	43	4	0	12 7	62	11	0
4 10	24	2	0	8 9	43	9	0	12 8	63	4	0
4 11	24	7	0	8 10	44	2	0	12 9	63	9	0
5 0	25	0	0	8 11	44	7	0	12 10	64	2	0
5 1	25	5	0	9 0	45	0	0	12 11	64	7	0
5 2	25	10	0	9 1	45	5	0	13 0	65	0	0
5 3	26	3	0	9 2	45	10	0				
5 4	26	8	0	9 3	46	3	0				

WITH RAILWAY SLIDES.

5-ft. 1-in.

5-ft. 1-in. by				5-ft. 1-in. by				5-ft. 1-in. by			
ft. in.	ft.	in.	pts.	ft. in.	ft.	in.	pts.	ft. in.	ft.	in.	pts.
1 6	= 7	7	6	5 5	=27	6	5	9 4	=47	5	4
1 7	8	0	7	5 6	27	11	6	9 5	47	10	5
1 8	8	5	8	5 7	28	4	7	9 6	48	3	6
1 9	8	10	9	5 8	28	9	8	9 7	48	8	7
1 10	9	3	10	5 9	29	2	9	9 8	49	1	8
1 11	9	8	11	5 10	29	7	10	9 9	49	6	9
2 0	10	2	0	5 11	30	0	11	9 10	49	11	10
2 1	10	7	1	6 0	30	6	0	9 11	50	4	11
2 2	11	0	2	6 1	30	11	1	10 0	50	10	0
2 3	11	5	3	6 2	31	4	2	10 1	51	3	1
2 4	11	10	4	6 3	31	9	3	10 2	51	8	2
2 5	12	3	5	6 4	32	2	4	10 3	52	1	3
2 6	12	8	6	6 5	32	7	5	10 4	52	6	4
2 7	13	1	7	6 6	33	0	6	10 5	52	11	5
2 8	13	6	8	6 7	33	5	7	10 6	53	4	6
2 9	13	11	9	6 8	33	10	8	10 7	53	9	7
2 10	14	4	10	6 9	34	3	9	10 8	54	2	8
2 11	14	9	11	6 10	34	8	10	10 9	54	7	9
3 0	15	3	0	6 11	35	1	11	10 10	55	0	10
3 1	15	8	1	7 0	35	7	0	10 11	55	5	11
3 2	16	1	2	7 1	36	0	1	11 0	55	11	0
3 3	16	6	3	7 2	36	5	2	11 1	56	4	1
3 4	16	11	4	7 3	36	10	3	11 2	56	9	2
3 5	17	4	5	7 4	37	3	4	11 3	57	2	3
3 6	17	9	6	7 5	37	8	5	11 4	57	7	4
3 7	18	2	7	7 6	38	1	6	11 5	58	0	5
3 8	18	7	8	7 7	38	6	7	11 6	58	5	6
3 9	19	0	9	7 8	38	11	8	11 7	58	10	7
3 10	19	5	10	7 9	39	4	9	11 8	59	3	8
3 11	19	10	11	7 10	39	9	10	11 9	59	8	9
4 0	20	4	0	7 11	40	2	11	11 10	60	1	10
4 1	20	9	1	8 0	40	8	0	11 11	60	6	11
4 2	21	2	2	8 1	41	1	1	12 0	61	0	0
4 3	21	7	3	8 2	41	6	2	12 1	61	5	1
4 4	22	0	4	8 3	41	11	3	12 2	61	10	2
4 5	22	5	5	8 4	42	4	4	12 3	62	3	3
4 6	22	10	6	8 5	42	9	5	12 4	62	8	4
4 7	23	3	7	8 6	43	2	6	12 5	63	1	5
4 8	23	8	8	8 7	43	7	7	12 6	63	6	6
4 9	24	1	9	8 8	44	0	8	12 7	63	11	7
4 10	24	6	10	8 9	44	5	9	12 8	64	4	8
4 11	24	11	11	8 10	44	10	10	12 9	64	9	9
5 0	25	5	0	8 11	45	3	11	12 10	65	2	10
5 1	25	10	1	9 0	45	9	0	12 11	65	7	11
5 2	26	3	2	9 1	46	2	1	13 0	66	1	0
5 3	26	8	3	9 2	46	7	2				
5 4	27	1	4	9 3	47	0	3				

5-ft. 2-in.

5-ft. 2-in. by				5-ft. 2-in. by				5-ft. 2-in. by			
ft.	in.	ft.	in. pts.	ft.	in.	ft.	in. pts.	ft.	in.	ft.	in. pts.
1	6	= 7	9 0	5	5	=27	11 10	9	4	=48	2 8
1	7	8	2 2	5	6	28	5 0	9	5	48	7 10
1	8	8	7 4	5	7	28	10 2	9	6	49	1 0
1	9	9	0 6	5	8	29	3 4	9	7	49	6 2
1	10	9	5 8	5	9	29	8 6	9	8	49	11 4
1	11	9	10 10	5	10	30	1 8	9	9	50	4 6
2	0	10	4 0	5	11	30	6 10	9	10	50	9 8
2	1	10	9 2	6	0	31	0 0	9	11	51	2 10
2	2	11	2 4	6	1	31	5 2	10	0	51	8 0
2	3	11	7 6	6	2	31	10 4	10	1	52	1 2
2	4	12	0 8	6	3	32	3 6	10	2	52	6 4
2	5	12	5 10	6	4	32	8 8	10	3	52	11 6
2	6	12	11 0	6	5	33	1 10	10	4	53	4 8
2	7	13	4 2	6	6	33	7 0	10	5	53	9 10
2	8	13	9 4	6	7	34	0 2	10	6	54	3 0
2	9	14	2 6	6	8	34	5 4	10	7	54	8 2
2	10	14	7 8	6	9	34	10 6	10	8	55	1 4
2	11	15	0 10	6	10	35	3 8	10	9	55	6 6
3	0	15	6 0	6	11	35	8 10	10	10	55	11 8
3	1	15	11 2	7	0	36	2 0	10	11	56	4 10
3	2	16	4 4	7	1	36	7 2	11	0	56	10 0
3	3	16	9 6	7	2	37	0 4	11	1	57	3 2
3	4	17	2 8	7	3	37	5 6	11	2	57	8 4
3	5	17	7 10	7	4	37	10 8	11	3	58	1 6
3	6	18	1 0	7	5	38	3 10	11	4	58	6 8
3	7	18	6 2	7	6	38	9 0	11	5	58	11 10
3	8	18	11 4	7	7	39	2 2	11	6	59	5 0
3	9	19	4 6	7	8	39	7 4	11	7	59	10 2
3	10	19	9 8	7	9	40	0 6	11	8	60	3 4
3	11	20	2 10	7	10	40	5 8	11	9	60	8 6
4	0.	20	8 0	7	11	40	10 10	11	10	61	1 8
4	1	21	1 2	8	0	41	4 0	11	11	61	6 10
4	2	21	6 4	8	1	41	9 2	12	0	62	0 0
4	3	21	11 6	8	2	42	2 4	12	1	62	5 2
4	4	22	4 8	8	3	42	7 6	12	2	62	10 4
4	5	22	9 10	8	4	43	0 8	12	3	63	3 6
4	6	23	3 0	8	5	43	5 10	12	4	63	8 8
4	7	23	8 2	8	6	43	11 0	12	5	64	1 10
4	8	24	1 4	8	7	44	4 2	12	6	64	7 0
4	9	24	6 6	8	8	44	9 4	12	7	65	0 2
4	10	24	11 8	8	9	45	2 6	12	8	65	5 4
4	11	25	4 10	8	10	45	7 8	12	9	65	10 6
5	0	25	10 0	8	11	46	0 10	12	10	66	3 8
5	1	26	3 2	9	0	46	6 0	12	11	66	8 10
5	2	26	8 4	9	1	46	11 2	13	0	67	2 0
5	3	27	1 6	9	2	47	4 4				
5	4	27	6 8	9	3	47	9 6				

5-ft. 3-in.

5-ft. 3-in. by				5-ft. 3-in. by				5-ft. 3-in. by		
ft. in.	ft.	in.	pts.	ft. in.	ft.	in.	pts.	ft. in.	ft.	in.	pts.
1 6	= 7	10	6	5 5	=28	5	3	9 4	=49	0	0
1 7	8	3	9	5 6	28	10	6	9 5	49	5	3
1 8	8	9	0	5 7	29	3	9	9 6	49	10	6
1 9	9	2	3	5 8	29	9	0	9 7	50	3	9
1 10	9	7	6	5 9	30	2	3	9 8	50	9	0
1 11	10	0	9	5 10	30	7	6	9 9	51	2	3
2 0	10	6	0	5 11	31	0	9	9 10	51	7	6
2 1	10	11	3	6 0	31	6	0	9 11	52	0	9
2 2	11	4	6	6 1	31	11	3	10 0	52	6	0
2 3	11	9	9	6 2	32	4	6	10 1	52	11	3
2 4	12	3	0	6 3	32	9	9	10 2	53	4	6
2 5	12	8	3	6 4	33	3	0	10 3	53	9	9
2 6	13	1	6	6 5	33	8	3	10 4	54	3	0
2 7	13	6	9	6 6	34	1	6	10 5	54	8	3
2 8	14	0	0	6 7	34	6	9	10 6	55	1	6
2 9	14	5	3	6 8	35	0	0	10 7	55	6	9
2 10	14	10	6	6 9	35	5	3	10 8	56	0	0
2 11	15	3	9	6 10	35	10	6	10 9	56	5	3
3 0	15	9	0	6 11	36	3	9	10 10	56	10	6
3 1	16	2	3	7 0	36	9	0	10 11	57	3	9
3 2	16	7	6	7 1	37	2	3	11 0	57	9	0
3 3	17	0	9	7 2	37	7	6	11 1	58	2	3
3 4	17	6	0	7 3	38	0	9	11 2	58	7	6
3 5	17	11	3	7 4	38	6	0	11 3	59	0	9
3 6	18	4	6	7 5	38	11	3	11 4	59	6	0
3 7	18	9	9	7 6	39	4	6	11 5	59	11	3
3 8	19	3	0	7 7	39	9	9	11 6	60	4	6
3 9	19	8	3	7 8	40	3	0	11 7	60	9	9
3 10	20	1	6	7 9	40	8	3	11 8	61	3	0
3 11	20	6	9	7 10	41	1	6	11 9	61	8	3
4 0	21	0	0	7 11	41	6	9	11 10	62	1	6
4 1	21	5	3	8 0	42	0	0	11 11	62	6	9
4 2	21	10	6	8 1	42	5	3	12 0	63	0	0
4 3	22	3	9	8 2	42	10	6	12 1	63	5	3
4 4	22	9	0	8 3	43	3	9	12 2	63	10	6
4 5	23	2	3	8 4	43	9	0	12 3	64	3	9
4 6	23	7	6	8 5	44	2	3	12 4	64	9	0
4 7	24	0	9	8 6	44	7	6	12 5	65	2	3
4 8	24	6	0	8 7	45	0	9	12 6	65	7	6
4 9	24	11	3	8 8	45	6	0	12 7	66	0	9
4 10	25	4	6	8 9	45	11	3	12 8	66	6	0
4 11	25	9	9	8 10	46	4	6	12 9	66	11	3
5 0	26	3	0	8 11	46	9	9	12 10	67	4	6
5 1	26	8	3	9 0	47	3	0	12 11	67	9	9
5 2	27	1	6	9 1	47	8	3	13 0	68	3	0
5 3	27	6	9	9 2	48	1	6				
5 4	28	0	0	9 3	48	6	9				

5-ft. 4-in.

ft. in.	ft. in. pts.	ft. in.	ft. in. pts.	ft. in.	ft. in. pts.
5-ft. 4-in. by		5-ft. 4-in. by		5-ft. 4-in. by	
1 6	= 8 0 0	5 5	= 28 10 8	9 4	= 49 9 4
1 7	8 5 4	5 6	29 4 0	9 5	50 2 8
1 8	8 10 8	5 7	29 9 4	9 6	50 8 0
1 9	9 4 0	5 8	30 2 8	9 7	51 1 4
1 10	9 9 4	5 9	30 8 0	9 8	51 6 8
1 11	10 2 8	5 10	31 1 4	9 9	52 0 0
2 0	10 8 0	5 11	31 6 8	9 10	52 5 4
2 1	11 1 4	6 0	32 0 0	9 11	52 10 8
2 2	11 6 8	6 1	32 5 4	10 0	53 4 0
2 3	12 0 0	6 2	32 10 8	10 1	53 9 4
2 4	12 5 4	6 3	33 4 0	10 2	54 2 8
2 5	12 10 8	6 4	33 9 4	10 3	54 8 0
2 6	13 4 0	6 5	34 2 8	10 4	55 1 4
2 7	13 9 4	6 6	34 8 0	10 5	55 6 8
2 8	14 2 8	6 7	35 1 4	10 6	56 0 0
2 9	14 8 0	6 8	35 6 8	10 7	56 5 4
2 10	15 1 4	6 9	36 0 0	10 8	56 10 8
2 11	15 6 8	6 10	36 5 4	10 9	57 4 0
3 0	16 0 0	6 11	36 10 8	10 10	57 9 4
3 1	16 5 4	7 0	37 4 0	10 11	58 2 8
3 2	16 10 8	7 1	37 9 4	11 0	58 8 0
3 3	17 4 0	7 2	38 2 8	11 1	59 1 4
3 4	17 9 4	7 3	38 8 0	11 2	59 6 8
3 5	18 2 8	7 4	39 1 4	11 3	60 0 0
3 6	18 8 0	7 5	39 6 8	11 4	60 5 4
3 7	19 1 4	7 6	40 0 0	11 5	60 10 8
3 8	19 6 8	7 7	40 5 4	11 6	61 4 0
3 9	20 0 0	7 8	40 10 8	11 7	61 9 4
3 10	20 5 4	7 9	41 4 0	11 8	62 2 8
3 11	20 10 8	7 10	41 9 4	11 9	62 8 0
4 0	21 4 0	7 11	42 2 8	11 10	63 1 4
4 1	21 9 4	8 0	42 8 0	11 11	63 6 8
4 2	22 2 8	8 1	43 1 4	12 0	64 0 0
4 3	22 8 0	8 2	43 6 8	12 1	64 5 4
4 4	23 1 4	8 3	44 0 0	12 2	64 10 8
4 5	23 6 8	8 4	44 5 4	12 3	65 4 0
4 6	24 0 0	8 5	44 10 8	12 4	65 9 4
4 7	24 5 4	8 6	45 4 0	12 5	66 2 8
4 8	24 10 8	8 7	45 9 4	12 6	66 8 0
4 9	25 4 0	8 8	46 2 8	12 7	67 1 4
4 10	25 9 4	8 9	46 8 0	12 8	67 6 8
4 11	26 2 8	8 10	47 1 4	12 9	68 0 0
5 0	26 8 0	8 11	47 6 8	12 10	68 5 4
5 1	27 1 4	9 0	48 0 0	12 11	68 10 8
5 2	27 6 8	9 1	48 5 4	13 0	69 4 0
5 3	28 0 0	9 2	48 10 8		
5 4	28 5 4	9 3	49 4 0		

ON AN IMPROVED PRINCIPLE.

5-ft. 5-in.

5-ft. 5-in. by				5-ft. 5-in. by				5-ft. 5-in. by			
ft.	in.	ft.	in. pts.	ft.	in.	ft	in. pts.	ft.	in.	ft.	in. pts.
1	6	= 8	1 6	5	5	=29	4 1	9	4	=50	6 8
1	7	8	6 11	5	6	29	9 6	9	5	51	0 1
1	8	9	0 4	5	7	30	2 11	9	6	51	5 6
1	9	9	5 9	5	8	30	8 4	9	7	51	10 11
1	10	9	11 2	5	9	31	1 9	9	8	52	4 4
1	11	10	4 7	5	10	31	7 2	9	9	52	9 9
2	0	10	10 0	5	11	32	0 7	9	10	53	3 2
2	1	11	3 5	6	0	32	6 0	9	11	53	8 7
2	2	11	8 10	6	1	32	11 5	10	0	54	2 0
2	3	12	2 3	6	2	33	4 10	10	1	54	7 5
2	4	12	7 8	6	3	33	10 3	10	2	55	0 10
2	5	13	1 1	6	4	34	3 8	10	3	55	6 3
2	6	13	6 6	6	5	34	9 1	10	4	55	11 8
2	7	13	11 11	6	6	35	2 6	10	5	56	5 1
2	8	14	5 4	6	7	35	7 11	10	6	56	10 6
2	9	14	10 9	6	8	36	1 4	10	7	57	3 11
2	10	15	4 2	6	9	36	6 9	10	8	57	9 4
2	11	15	9 7	6	10	37	0 2	10	9	58	2 9
3	0	16	3 0	6	11	37	5 7	10	10	58	8 2
3	1	16	8 5	7	0	37	11 0	10	11	59	1 7
3	2	17	1 10	7	1	38	4 5	11	0	59	7 0
3	3	17	7 3	7	2	38	9 10	11	1	60	0 5
3	4	18	0 8	7	3	39	3 3	11	2	60	5 10
3	5	18	6 1	7	4	39	8 8	11	3	60	11 3
3	6	18	11 6	7	5	40	2 1	11	4	61	4 8
3	7	19	4 11	7	6	40	7 6	11	5	61	10 1
3	8	19	10 4	7	7	41	0 11	11	6	62	3 6
3	9	20	3 9	7	8	41	6 4	11	7	62	8 11
3	10	20	9 2	7	9	41	11 9	11	8	63	2 4
3	11	21	2 7	7	10	42	5 2	11	9	63	7 9
4	0	21	8 0	7	11	42	10 7	11	10	64	1 2
4	1	22	1 5	8	0	43	4 0	11	11	64	6 7
4	2	22	6 10	8	1	43	9 5	12	0	65	0 0
4	3	23	0 3	8	2	44	2 10	12	1	65	5 5
4	4	23	5 8	8	3	44	8 3	12	2	65	10 10
4	5	23	11 1	8	4	45	1 8	12	3	66	4 3
4	6	24	4 6	8	5	45	7 1	12	4	66	9 8
4	7	24	9 11	8	6	46	0 6	12	5	67	3 1
4	8	25	3 4	8	7	46	5 11	12	6	67	8 6
4	9	25	8 9	8	8	46	11 4	12	7	68	1 11
4	10	26	2 2	8	9	47	4 9	12	8	68	7 4
4	11	26	7 7	8	10	47	10 2	12	9	69	0 9
5	0	27	1 0	8	11	48	3 7	12	10	69	6 2
5	1	27	6 5	9	0	48	9 0	12	11	69	11 7
5	2	27	11 10	9	1	49	2 5	13	0	70	5 0
5	3	28	5 3	9	2	49	7 10				
5	4	28	10 8	9	3	50	1 3				

5-ft. 6-in.

5-ft. 6-in. by				5-ft. 6-in. by				5-ft. 6-in. by			
ft. in.	ft.	in.	pts.	ft. in.	ft.	in.	pts.	ft. in.	ft.	in.	pts.
1 6	= 8	3	0	5 5	=29	9	6	9 4	=51	4	0
1 7	8	8	6	5 6	30	3	0	9 5	51	9	6
1 8	9	2	0	5 7	30	8	6	9 6	52	3	0
1 9	9	7	6	5 8	31	2	0	9 7	52	8	6
1 10	10	1	0	5 9	31	7	6	9 8	53	2	0
1 11	10	6	6	5 10	32	1	0	9 9	53	7	6
2 0	11	0	0	5 11	32	6	6	9 10	54	1	0
2 1	11	5	6	6 0	33	0	0	9 11	54	6	6
2 2	11	11	0	6 1	33	5	6	10 0	55	0	0
2 3	12	4	6	6 2	33	11	0	10 1	55	5	6
2 4	12	10	0	6 3	34	4	6	10 2	55	11	0
2 5	13	3	6	6 4	34	10	0	10 3	56	4	6
2 6	13	9	0	6 5	35	3	6	10 4	56	10	0
2 7	14	2	6	6 6	35	9	0	10 5	57	3	6
2 8	14	8	0	6 7	36	2	6	10 6	57	9	0
2 9	15	1	6	6 8	36	8	0	10 7	58	2	6
2 10	15	7	0	6 9	37	1	6	10 8	58	8	0
2 11	16	0	6	6 10	37	7	0	10 9	59	1	6
3 0	16	6	0	6 11	38	0	6	10 10	59	7	0
3 1	16	11	6	7 0	38	6	0	10 11	60	0	6
3 2	17	5	0	7 1	38	11	6	11 0	60	6	0
3 3	17	10	6	7 2	39	5	0	11 1	60	11	6
3 4	18	4	0	7 3	39	10	6	11 2	61	5	0
3 5	18	9	6	7 4	40	4	0	11 3	61	10	6
3 6	19	3	0	7 5	40	9	6	11 4	62	4	0
3 7	19	8	6	7 6	41	3	0	11 5	62	9	6
3 8	20	2	0	7 7	41	8	6	11 6	63	3	0
3 9	20	7	6	7 8	42	2	0	11 7	63	8	6
3 10	21	1	0	7 9	42	7	6	11 8	64	2	0
3 11	21	6	6	7 10	43	1	0	11 9	64	7	6
4 0	22	0	0	7 11	43	6	6	11 10	65	1	0
4 1	22	5	6	8 0	44	0	0	11 11	65	6	6
4 2	22	11	0	8 1	44	5	6	12 0	66	0	0
4 3	23	4	6	8 2	44	11	0	12 1	66	5	6
4 4	23	10	0	8 3	45	4	6	12 2	66	11	0
4 5	24	3	6	8 4	45	10	0	12 3	67	4	6
4 6	24	9	0	8 5	46	3	6	12 4	67	10	0
4 7	25	2	6	8 6	46	9	0	12 5	68	3	6
4 8	25	8	0	8 7	47	2	6	12 6	68	9	0
4 9	26	1	6	8 8	47	8	0	12 7	69	2	6
4 10	26	7	0	8 9	48	1	6	12 8	69	8	0
4 11	27	0	6	8 10	48	7	0	12 9	70	1	6
5 0	27	6	0	8 11	49	0	6	12 10	70	7	0
5 1	27	11	6	9 0	49	6	0	12 11	71	0	6
5 2	28	5	0	9 1	49	11	6	13 0	71	6	0
5 3	28	10	6	9 2	50	5	0				
5 4	29	4	0	9 3	50	10	6				

FOR GARDEN ENTRANCES.

5-ft. 7-in.

5-ft. 7-in. by				5-ft. 7-in. by				5-ft. 7-in. by		
ft. in.	ft.	in.	pts.	ft. in.	ft.	in.	pts.	ft. in.	ft.	in.	pts.
1 6	= 8	4	6	5 5	=30	2	11	9 4	=52	1	4
1 7	8	10	1	5 6	30	8	6	9 5	52	6	11
1 8	9	3	8	5 7	31	2	1	9 6	53	0	6
1 9	9	9	3	5 8	31	7	8	9 7	53	6	1
1 10	10	2	10	5 9	32	1	3	9 8	53	11	8
1 11	10	8	5	5 10	32	6	10	9 9	54	5	3
2 0	11	2	0	5 11	33	0	5	9 10	54	10	10
2 1	11	7	7	6 0	33	6	0	9 11	55	4	5
2 2	12	1	2	6 1	33	11	7	10 0	55	10	0
2 3	12	6	9	6 2	34	5	2	10 1	56	3	7
2 4	13	0	4	6 3	34	10	9	10 2	56	9	2
2 5	13	5	11	6 4	35	4	4	10 3	57	2	9
2 6	13	11	6	6 5	35	9	11	10 4	57	8	4
2 7	14	5	1	6 6	36	3	6	10 5	58	1	11
2 8	14	10	8	6 7	36	9	1	10 6	58	7	6
2 9	15	4	3	6 8	37	2	8	10 7	59	1	1
2 10	15	9	10	6 9	37	8	3	10 8	59	6	8
2 11	16	3	5	6 10	38	1	10	10 9	60	0	3
3 0	16	9	0	6 11	38	7	5	10 10	60	5	10
3 1	17	2	7	7 0	39	1	0	10 11	60	11	5
3 2	17	8	2	7 1	39	6	7	11 0	61	5	0
3 3	18	1	9	7 2	40	0	2	11 1	61	10	7
3 4	18	7	4	7 3	40	5	9	11 2	62	4	2
3 5	19	0	11	7 4	40	11	4	11 3	62	9	9
3 6	19	6	6	7 5	41	4	11	11 4	63	3	4
3 7	20	0	1	7 6	41	10	6	11 5	63	8	11
3 8	20	5	8	7 7	42	4	1	11 6	64	2	6
3 9	20	11	3	7 8	42	9	8	11 7	64	8	1
3 10	21	4	10	7 9	43	3	3	11 8	65	1	8
3 11	21	10	5	7 10	43	8	10	11 9	65	7	3
4 0	22	4	0	7 11	44	2	5	11 10	66	0	10
4 1	22	9	7	8 0	44	8	0	11 11	66	6	5
4 2	23	3	2	8 1	45	1	7	12 0	67	0	0
4 3	23	8	9	8 2	45	7	2	12 1	67	5	7
4 4	24	2	4	8 3	46	0	9	12 2	67	11	2
4 5	24	7	11	8 4	46	6	4	12 3	68	4	9
4 6	25	1	6	8 5	46	11	11	12 4	68	10	4
4 7	25	7	1	8 6	47	5	6	12 5	69	3	11
4 8	26	0	8	8 7	47	11	1	12 6	69	9	6
4 9	26	6	3	8 8	48	4	8	12 7	70	3	1
4 10	26	11	10	8 9	48	10	3	12 8	70	8	8
4 11	27	5	5	8 10	49	3	10	12 9	71	2	3
5 0	27	11	0	8 11	49	9	5	12 10	71	7	10
5 1	28	4	7	9 0	50	3	0	12 11	72	1	5
5 2	28	10	2	9 1	50	8	7	13 0	72	7	0
5 3	29	3	9	9 2	51	2	2				
5 4	29	9	4	9 3	51	7	9				

5-ft. 8-in.

5-ft. 8-in. by			5-ft. 8-in. by			5-ft. 8-in. by		
ft. in.	ft. in. pts.		ft. in.	ft. in. pts.		ft. in.	ft. in. pts.	
1 6	= 8 6 0		5 5	=30 8 4		9 4	=52 10 8	
1 7	8 11 8		5 6	31 2 0		9 5	53 4 4	
1 8	9 5 4		5 7	31 7 8		9 6	53 10 0	
1 9	9 11 0		5 8	32 1 4		9 7	54 3 8	
1 10	10 4 8		5 9	32 7 0		9 8	54 9 4	
1 11	10 10 4		5 10	33 0 8		9 9	55 3 0	
2 0	11 4 0		5 11	33 6 4		9 10	55 8 8	
2 1	11 9 8		6 0	34 0 0		9 11	56 2 4	
2 2	12 3 4		6 1	34 5 8		10 0	56 8 0	
2 3	12 9 0		6 2	34 11 4		10 1	57 1 8	
2 4	13 2 8		6 3	35 5 0		10 2	57 7 4	
2 5	13 8 4		6 4	35 10 8		10 3	58 1 0	
2 6	14 2 0		6 5	36 4 4		10 4	58 6 8	
2 7	14 7 8		6 6	36 10 0		10 5	59 0 4	
2 8	15 1 4		6 7	37 3 8		10 6	59 6 0	
2 9	15 7 0		6 8	37 9 4		10 7	59 11 8	
2 10	16 0 8		6 9	38 3 0		10 8	60 5 4	
2 11	16 6 4		6 10	38 8 8		10 9	60 11 0	
3 0	17 0 0		6 11	39 2 4		10 10	61 4 8	
3 1	17 5 8		7 0	39 8 0		10 11	61 10 4	
3 2	17 11 4		7 1	40 1 8		11 0	62 4 0	
3 3	18 5 0		7 2	40 7 4		11 1	62 9 8	
3 4	18 10 8		7 3	41 1 0		11 2	63 3 4	
3 5	19 4 4		7 4	41 6 8		11 3	63 9 0	
3 6	19 10 0		7 5	42 0 4		11 4	64 2 8	
3 7	20 3 8		7 6	42 6 0		11 5	64 8 4	
3 8	20 9 4		7 7	42 11 8		11 6	65 2 0	
3 9	21 3 0		7 8	43 5 4		11 7	65 7 8	
3 10	21 8 8		7 9	43 11 0		11 8	66 1 4	
3 11	22 2 4		7 10	44 4 8		11 9	66 7 0	
4 0	22 8 0		7 11	44 10 4		11 10	67 0 8	
4 1	23 1 8		8 0	45 4 0		11 11	67 6 4	
4 2	23 7 4		8 1	45 9 8		12 0	68 0 0	
4 3	24 1 0		8 2	46 3 4		12 1	68 5 8	
4 4	24 6 8		8 3	46 9 0		12 2	68 11 4	
4 5	25 0 4		8 4	47 2 8		12 3	69 5 0	
4 6	25 6 0		8 5	47 8 4		12 4	69 10 8	
4 7	25 11 8		8 6	48 2 0		12 5	70 4 4	
4 8	26 5 4		8 7	48 7 8		12 6	70 10 0	
4 9	26 11 0		8 8	49 1 4		12 7	71 3 8	
4 10	27 4 8		8 9	49 7 0		12 8	71 9 4	
4 11	27 10 4		8 10	50 0 8		12 9	72 3 0	
5 0	28 4 0		8 11	50 6 4		12 10	72 8 8	
5 1	28 9 8		9 0	51 0 0		12 11	73 2 4	
5 2	29 3 4		9 1	51 5 8		13 0	73 8 0	
5 3	29 9 0		9 2	51 11 4				
5 4	30 2 8		9 3	52 5 0				

AND PATTERNS SENT.

5-ft. 9-in.

ft. in.	ft.	in.	pts.	ft. in.	ft.	in.	pts.	ft. in.	ft.	in.	pts.
1 6	= 8	7	6	5 5	=31	1	9	9 4	=53	8	0
1 7	9	1	3	5 6	31	7	6	9 5	54	1	9
1 8	9	7	0	5 7	32	1	3	9 6	54	7	6
1 9	10	0	9	5 8	32	7	0	9 7	55	1	3
1 10	10	6	6	5 9	33	0	9	9 8	55	7	0
1 11	11	0	3	5 10	33	6	6	9 9	56	0	9
2 0	11	6	0	5 11	34	0	3	9 10	56	6	6
2 1	11	11	9	6 0	34	6	0	9 11	57	0	3
2 2	12	5	6	6 1	34	11	9	10 0	57	6	0
2 3	12	11	3	6 2	35	5	6	10 1	57	11	9
2 4	13	5	0	6 3	35	11	3	10 2	58	5	6
2 5	13	10	9	6 4	36	5	0	10 3	58	11	3
2 6	14	4	6	6 5	36	10	9	10 4	59	5	0
2 7	14	10	3	6 6	37	4	6	10 5	59	10	9
2 8	15	4	0	6 7	37	10	3	10 6	60	4	6
2 9	15	9	9	6 8	38	4	0	10 7	60	10	3
2 10	16	3	6	6 9	38	9	9	10 8	61	4	0
2 11	16	9	3	6 10	39	3	6	10 9	61	9	9
3 0	17	3	0	6 11	39	9	3	10 10	62	3	6
3 1	17	8	9	7 0	40	3	0	10 11	62	9	3
3 2	18	2	6	7 1	40	8	9	11 0	63	3	0
3 3	18	8	3	7 2	41	2	6	11 1	63	8	9
3 4	19	2	0	7 3	41	8	3	11 2	64	2	6
3 5	19	7	9	7 4	42	2	0	11 3	64	8	3
3 6	20	1	6	7 5	42	7	9	11 4	65	2	0
3 7	20	7	3	7 6	43	1	6	11 5	65	7	9
3 8	21	1	0	7 7	43	7	3	11 6	66	1	6
3 9	21	6	9	7 8	44	1	0	11 7	66	7	3
3 10	22	0	6	7 9	44	6	9	11 8	67	1	0
3 11	22	6	3	7 10	45	0	6	11 9	67	6	9
4 0	23	0	0	7 11	45	6	3	11 10	68	0	6
4 1	23	5	9	8 0	46	0	0	11 11	68	6	3
4 2	23	11	6	8 1	46	5	9	12 0	69	0	0
4 3	24	5	3	8 2	46	11	6	12 1	69	5	9
4 4	24	11	0	8 3	47	5	3	12 2	69	11	6
4 5	25	4	9	8 4	47	11	0	12 3	70	5	3
4 6	25	10	6	8 5	48	4	9	12 4	70	11	0
4 7	26	4	3	8 6	48	10	6	12 5	71	4	9
4 8	26	10	0	8 7	49	4	3	12 6	71	10	6
4 9	27	3	9	8 8	49	10	0	12 7	72	4	3
4 10	27	9	6	8 9	50	3	9	12 8	72	10	0
4 11	28	3	3	8 10	50	9	6	12 9	73	3	9
5 0	28	9	0	8 11	51	3	3	12 10	73	9	6
5 1	29	2	9	9 0	51	9	0	12 11	74	3	3
5 2	29	8	6	9 1	52	2	9	13 0	74	9	0
5 3	30	2	3	9 2	52	8	6				
5 4	30	8	0	9 3	53	2	3				

5-ft. 10-in.

5-ft. 10-in. by				5-ft. 10-in. by				5-ft. 10-in. by			
ft.	in.	ft. in. pts.		ft.	in.	ft. in. pts.		ft.	in.	ft. in. pts.	
1	6	= 8 9 0		5	5	=31 7 2		9	4	=54 5 4	
1	7	9 2 10		5	6	32 1 0		9	5	54 11 2	
1	8	9 8 8		5	7	32 6 10		9	6	55 5 0	
1	9	10 2 6		5	8	33 0 8		9	7	55 10 10	
1	10	10 8 4		5	9	33 6 6		9	8	56 4 8	
1	11	11 2 2		5	10	34 0 4		9	9	56 10 6	
2	0	11 8 0		5	11	34 6 2		9	10	57 4 4	
2	1	12 1 10		6	0	35 0 0		9	11	57 10 2	
2	2	12 7 8		6	1	35 5 10		10	0	58 4 0	
2	3	13 1 6		6	2	35 11 8		10	1	58 9 10	
2	4	13 7 4		6	3	36 5 6		10	2	59 3 8	
2	5	14 1 2		6	4	36 11 4		10	3	59 9 6	
2	6	14 7 0		6	5	37 5 2		10	4	60 3 4	
2	7	15 0 10		6	6	37 11 0		10	5	60 9 2	
2	8	15 6 8		6	7	38 4 10		10	6	61 3 0	
2	9	16 0 6		6	8	38 10 8		10	7	61 8 10	
2	10	16 6 4		6	9	39 4 6		10	8	62 2 8	
2	11	17 0 2		6	10	39 10 4		10	9	62 8 6	
3	0	17 6 0		6	11	40 4 2		10	10	63 2 4	
3	1	17 11 10		7	0	40 10 0		10	11	63 8 2	
3	2	18 5 8		7	1	41 3 10		11	0	64 2 0	
3	3	18 11 6		7	2	41 9 8		11	1	64 7 10	
3	4	19 5 4		7	3	42 3 6		11	2	65 1 8	
3	5	19 11 2		7	4	42 9 4		11	3	65 7 6	
3	6	20 5 0		7	5	43 3 2		11	4	66 1 4	
3	7	20 10 10		7	6	43 9 0		11	5	66 7 2	
3	8	21 4 8		7	7	44 2 10		11	6	67 1 0	
3	9	21 10 6		7	8	44 8 8		11	7	67 6 10	
3	10	22 4 4		7	9	45 2 6		11	8	68 0 8	
3	11	22 10 2		7	10	45 8 4		11	9	68 6 6	
4	0	23 4 0		7	11	46 2 2		11	10	69 0 4	
4	1	23 9 10		8	0	46 8 0		11	11	69 6 2	
4	2	24 3 8		8	1	47 1 10		12	0	70 0 0	
4	3	24 9 6		8	2	47 7 8		12	1	70 5 10	
4	4	25 3 4		8	3	48 1 6		12	2	70 11 8	
4	5	25 9 2		8	4	48 7 4		12	3	71 5 6	
4	6	26 3 0		8	5	49 1 2		12	4	71 11 4	
4	7	26 8 10		8	6	49 7 0		12	5	72 5 2	
4	8	27 2 8		8	7	50 0 10		12	6	72 11 0	
4	9	27 8 6		8	8	50 6 8		12	7	73 4 10	
4	10	28 2 4		8	9	51 0 6		12	8	73 10 8	
4	11	28 8 2		8	10	51 6 4		12	9	74 4 6	
5	0	29 2 0		8	11	52 0 2		12	10	74 10 4	
5	1	29 7 10		9	0	52 6 0		12	11	75 4 2	
5	2	30 1 8		9	1	52 11 10		13	0	75 10 0	
5	3	30 7 6		9	2	53 5 8					
5	4	31 1 4		9	3	53 11 6					

TO VERANDAHS AND PORTICOES.

5-ft. 11-in.

5-ft. 11-in. by				5-ft. 11-in. by				5-ft. 11-in. by		
ft. in.	ft.	in.	pts.	ft. in.	ft.	in.	pts.	ft. in.	ft.	in.	pts.
1 6	= 8	10	6	5 5	=32	0	7	9 4	=55	2	8
1 7	9	4	5	5 6	32	6	6	9 5	55	8	7
1 8	9	10	4	5 7	33	0	5	9 6	56	2	6
1 9	10	4	3	5 8	33	6	4	9 7	56	8	5
1 10	10	10	2	5 9	34	0	3	9 8	57	2	4
1 11	11	4	1	5 10	34	6	2	9 9	57	8	3
2 0	11	10	0	5 11	35	0	1	9 10	58	2	2
2 1	12	3	11	6 0	35	6	0	9 11	58	8	1
2 2	12	9	10	6 1	35	11	11	10 0	59	2	0
2 3	13	3	9	6 2	36	5	10	10 1	59	7	11
2 4	13	9	8	6 3	36	11	9	10 2	60	1	10
2 5	14	3	7	6 4	37	5	8	10 3	60	7	9
2 6	14	9	6	6 5	37	11	7	10 4	61	1	8
2 7	15	3	5	6 6	38	5	6	10 5	61	7	7
2 8	15	9	4	6 7	38	11	5	10 6	62	1	6
2 9	16	3	3	6 8	39	5	4	10 7	62	7	5
2 10	16	9	2	6 9	39	11	3	10 8	63	1	4
2 11	17	3	1	6 10	40	5	2	10 9	63	7	3
3 0	17	9	0	6 11	40	11	1	10 10	64	1	2
3 1	18	2	11	7 0	41	5	0	10 11	64	7	1
3 2	18	8	10	7 1	41	10	11	11 0	65	1	0
3 3	19	2	9	7 2	42	4	10	11 1	65	6	11
3 4	19	8	8	7 3	42	10	9	11 2	66	0	10
3 5	20	2	7	7 4	43	4	8	11 3	66	6	9
3 6	20	8	6	7 5	43	10	7	11 4	67	0	8
3 7	21	2	5	7 6	44	4	6	11 5	67	6	7
3 8	21	8	4	7 7	44	10	5	11 6	68	0	6
3 9	22	2	3	7 8	45	4	4	11 7	68	6	5
3 10	22	8	2	7 9	45	10	3	11 8	69	0	4
3 11	23	2	1	7 10	46	4	2	11 9	69	6	3
4 0	23	8	0	7 11	46	10	1	11 10	70	0	2
4 1	24	1	11	8 0	47	4	0	11 11	70	6	1
4 2	24	7	10	8 1	47	9	11	12 0	71	0	0
4 3	25	1	9	8 2	48	3	10	12 1	71	5	11
4 4	25	7	8	8 3	48	9	9	12 2	71	11	10
4 5	26	1	7	8 4	49	3	8	12 3	72	5	9
4 6	26	7	6	8 5	49	9	7	12 4	72	11	8
4 7	27	1	5	8 6	50	3	6	12 5	73	5	7
4 8	27	7	4	8 7	50	9	5	12 6	73	11	6
4 9	28	1	3	8 8	51	3	4	12 7	74	5	5
4 10	28	7	2	8 9	51	9	3	12 8	74	11	4
4 11	29	1	1	8 10	52	3	2	12 9	75	5	3
5 0	29	7	0	8 11	52	9	1	12 10	75	11	2
5 1	30	0	11	9 0	53	3	0	12 11	76	5	1
5 2	30	6	10	9 1	53	8	11	13 0	76	11	0
5 3	31	0	9	9 2	54	2	10				
5 4	31	6	8	9 3	54	8	9				

VENETIAN BLINDS.

OUR VENETIAN BLINDS are made of the best American Pine, painted in the best manner, and in some colours varnished, with Tapes of the best super linen webbing made expressly for us.

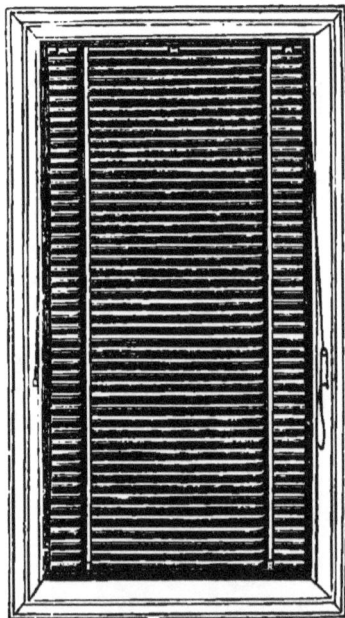

Venetian Blinds of selected Pine, clear varnished, showing the natural colour of the wood, or slightly stained satin-wood or walnut colour, have a very handsome appearance, besides being lighter than painted blinds. The Laths are carefully selected, so that no stain or discoloration may appear.

The Patent Actions are strongly recommended.

C. COLLYER & SON,

WINDOW BLIND MANUFACTURERS,

36, FARRINGDON STREET, LONDON, E.C.

Established 1742.

SPRING BLINDS.

THE new Striped Holland lately introduced has found great favour in this Country, from the variety of tasteful patterns suitable to various styles of buildings. We were the first in London to use it, and have a large stock of various colours and designs.

There is a certain prejudice in many quarters against Spring Blinds from the springs so often being improperly made, thus requiring frequent repair and being a constant source of annoyance, but if properly made they will last for years without getting out of order.

We guarantee the working of our springs. Some we put up thirty years ago are in constant use and work well now.

OUTSIDE FLORENTINE BLIND.

THIS form of Outside Blind is specially suitable for Casement Windows opening outwards, as the Casements can be opened when the Blind is down; also in the case of Sash Windows, they permit of ample ventilation either from the top or bottom of the Window.

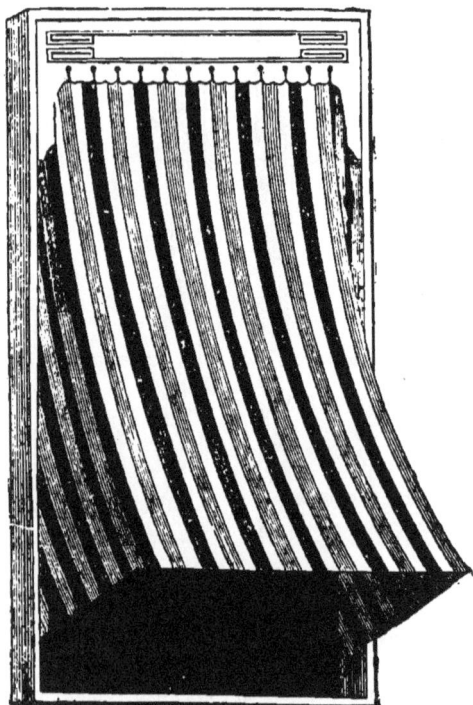

C. COLLYER & SON,
WINDOW BLIND MANUFACTURERS,
36, FARRINGDON STREET, LONDON, E.C.

Established 1742.

IMPROVED SPANISH BLINDS.

A S the usual form of Spanish Blinds with side wings, as shown in the Illustration, is sometimes objected to, we make them when required without the side gussets, so that the side wings on the case are unnecessary. The fascia then does not exclude nearly so much light from the window as it does with the side wings.

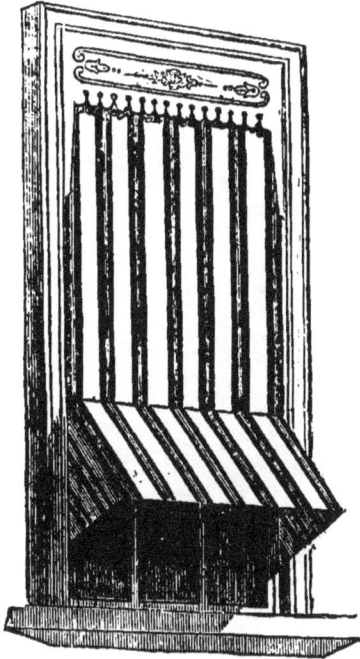

Where the architectural features of the building do not admit of wooden jambs to the cases of Spanish blinds, we make them with iron tubes for the runners to work in, fixed to the front lining of the sash frame. The slight additional cost of these is amply repaid by the neat appearance they present.

C. COLLYER & SON,
WINDOW BLIND MANUFACTURERS,
36, FARRINGDON STREET, LONDON, E.C.

Established 1742.

OUTSIDE SHUTTER BLINDS.

THE best form of Outside Shutter Blinds are the Sliding Railway Shutters, as they are much stronger, being supported throughout their whole width, and with the improved gun-metal runners which we have introduced for the top and bottom, they work with the greatest possible ease and absence of friction, so much so that, if desired, they can be made to work with cords brought by pulleys through the wall into the room.

Estimates given for fitting up either hinged or sliding shutter blinds in any part of the country.

C. COLLYER & SON,
WINDOW BLIND MANUFACTURERS,
36, FARRINGDON STREET, LONDON, E.C.

Established 1742.

HELIOSCENE BLIND.

THE advantage of the Helioscene Blind is, that when down it affords an unobstructed view between the boards, besides admitting air freely.

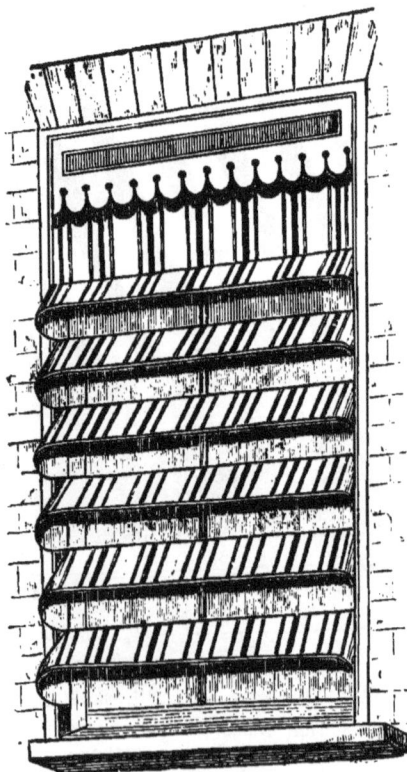

C. COLLYER & SON,
WINDOW BLIND MANUFACTURERS,
36, FARRINGDON STREET, LONDON, E.C.

Established 1742.

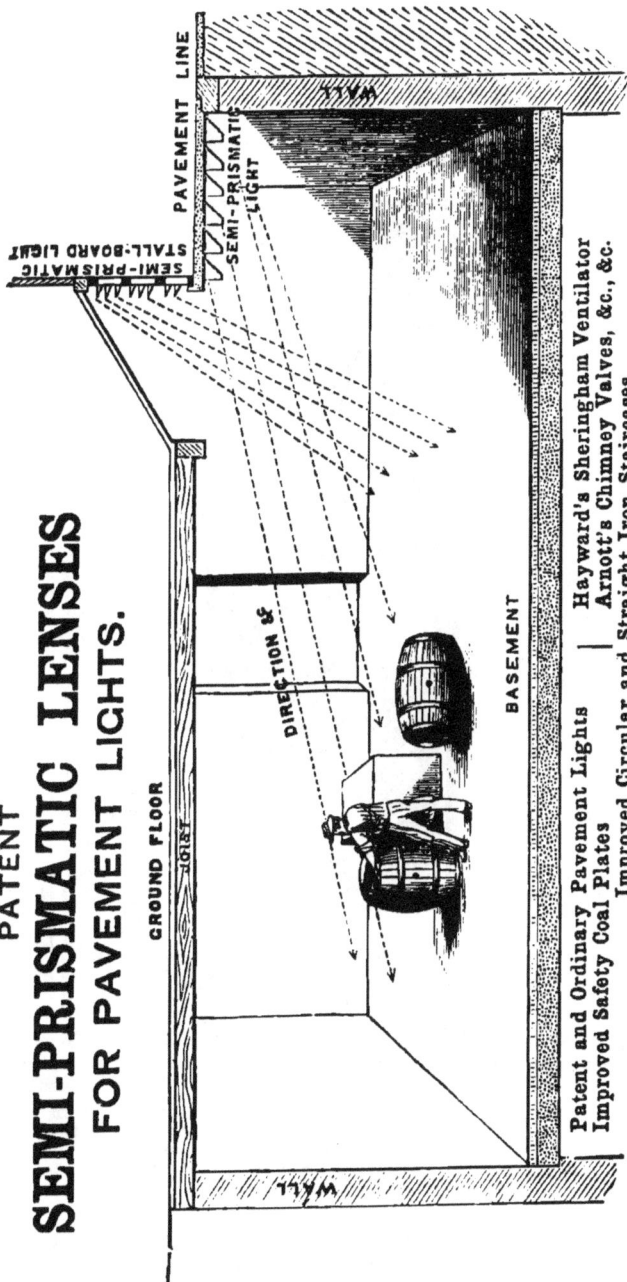

www.ingramcontent.com/pod-product-compliance
Lightning Source LLC
Chambersburg PA
CBHW022145090426
42742CB00010B/1396